NATHAN O. HATCH

The Sacred Cause of Liberty

Republican Thought and the Millennium
in Revolutionary New England

New Haven & London
Yale University Press: 1977

Published with assistance from
the Mary Cady Tew Memorial Fund.

Designed by Thos Whitridge
and set in Sabon type.
Printed in the United States of America by
Vail-Ballou Press, Binghamton, N.Y.

Published in Great Britain, Europe, Africa, and Asia
(except Japan) by Yale University Press, Ltd., London.
Distributed in Latin America by Kaiman & Polon, Inc.,
New York City; in Australia and New Zealand by Book & Film
Services, Artarmon, N.S.W., Australia; and in Japan
by Harper & Row, Publishers, Tokyo Office.

Library of Congress Cataloging in Publication Data

Hatch, Nathan O.
    The sacred cause of liberty.

    Bibliography: p.
    Includes index.
    1. Religious thought—New England. 2. Political
science—New England. 3. Millennialism. 4. Clergy—New England. I. Title.
BR520.H34   261.7'0974   77-76299
ISBN 0-300-02092-9

For Julie

Contents

Acknowledgments

It was a rare privilege to be introduced to the serious study of the eighteenth century by Professors John M. Murrin and J. G. A. Pocock. In complementary ways, both possess the talent for inspiring students to come to grips with the past on its own terms: Pocock by posing in numerous forms the question, "What was it possible for a given historical person or persons to think?" Murrin by unmasking as temporary fashion much that has seemed certain about eighteenth-century America. Both have treated their students with tremendous respect and have given unsparingly of their time and encouragement. I shall never forget the thoughtfulness of John Murrin in reading and criticizing the first chapter of this study on the same hot summer day that he and Mary were in the throes of moving from St. Louis to Princeton. I owe a considerable debt, as well, to the lively intellectual community I found in the history department of Washington University from 1970 to 1974.

Professor Timothy L. Smith of the Johns Hopkins University went the second mile to ensure that a post-doctoral fellowship under his direction would provide the time necessary to transform a dissertation into a book. If I have failed to kill off the "academese" in this work, it is because I have paid too little attention to his trenchant criticism of content and style. In the course of my thinking about republican thought and the millennium, a number of other scholars have offered crucial advice and assistance, among them: Michael McGiffert, C. C. Goen, John F. Wilson, Rhys Isaac, Lance Banning, Martin E. Marty, George M. Marsden, James W. Davidson, and Mark A. Noll. I am

X   ACKNOWLEDGMENTS

also grateful for the congenial atmosphere and genuine respect for scholarship I have enjoyed in the history department of the University of Notre Dame, where this work was brought to completion.

Also in order is a special word of thanks to the American Antiquarian Society for making available the microprint collection *Early American Imprints, 1639–1800;* to the audio-visual departments of the libraries at Washington University, the Johns Hopkins University, and the University of Notre Dame, where the lion's share of this research has been done; to the staff of the Congregational Library in Boston for splendid advice; to the *William and Mary Quarterly* for permission to reprint a revised version of an earlier article; to Elizabeth Gregg and Mrs. Vincent P. Gregg, Sr., who cheerfully read and criticized more versions of this work than I care to remember; and to Edward Tripp, Catherine Iino, and Marya Holcombe for their excellent cooperation and expert editorial advice. This research would have been impossible without the generous financial assistance of the Ford Foundation, the Lilly Endowment, and the American Council of Learned Societies.

In my parents I saw a deep regard for ideas and a sense of the importance of being intellectually self-conscious. My father always resisted being taken in by the local errors of his own time and place and I am grateful for his example. My appreciation of men like Jonathan Edwards, who refused to abide the whims of his own day, is evidence of my father's commitment to being in the world but not of it.

My greatest debt is to my wife Julie, who has supported me with unfailing encouragement and patience. She has always possessed a rare talent for recognizing quality and deflating pretension and no less so in trying to harness my speculations to good purpose. This is the seventh year that

Julie has heard me ramble on about how people in the past studied the future and she richly deserves a sabbatical. Gregg, I hope that by the time you can read this, dad will take more time for the present.

Indeed, the sacred cause of liberty hath been, and ever will be venerable in every part of the world where knowledge, and learning flourish, and men suffered to think and speak for themselves. Yea, it must be added, that Heaven hath appeared in the cause of liberty, and that in the most open and decisive manner: For this, the Son of God was manifest in the flesh, that he might destroy the tyranny of sin and satan, assert and maintain the equal government of his Father, redeem the guilty slaves from their more than Egyptian bondage, and cause the oppressed to go free.

Levi Hart, 1775

Introduction

Parson [Samuel] West was a much more consistent Whig than his patron and classmate, John Hancock, for although he regarded theological heresy as a possibly useful exploration of the nature of God, he could not tolerate Loyalism.

Clifford K. Shipton

By 1747 Jonathan Edwards carried a heavy burden. As New England's most articulate champion of vital religion, he was keenly sensitive to the cloud of spiritual darkness that had veiled the brightness of the Great Awakening. Dismayed that "infidelity, heresy and vice" had risen to such crisis proportions, Edwards joined a group of Scottish divines in calling for "an express *agreement,* unitedly to pray to God in an extraordinary manner, that he would . . . *pour out his spirit, revive his work,* and advance his spiritual kingdom in the world, as he promised." His program for initiating the kingdom of God in church and state was concerted prayer for a revival that would spread "till *whole nations* be awakened, and there be at length an accession of many of the chief nations of the world to the church of God."[1]

Edwards was certainly not the first or the last Yankee minister to propose that New England, by exerting her collective will, could actually bend the shape of history into the form ordained by Providence. Nor does his *Humble Attempt* stand as an isolated suggestion that a concert of

---

1. Jonathan Edwards, *The Works of President Edwards,* reprint ed. New York, 1968 (orig. publ. London, 1817), 2:478, 436–437.

I

prayer might be the very means to accomplish such a re-alignment of human and divine wills. Forty years later, in 1787, a group of ministers in Exeter, New Hampshire, renewed this technique to express their equally grave diagnosis of the moral condition of their countrymen and to suggest an appropriate cure. "How has luxury prevailed," they declared, "and every iniquity, every moral evil, abounded among us!" Like Edwards they suggested that men join in a united effort to reverse this alarming moral decay. But the object of the prayer which they suggested for such gatherings had faint resemblance to that to which the petitions of Edwards were directed. In addition to the necessity of renewed piety, these ministers called for incessant prayer that "the spirit of true republican government may universally pervade the citizens of the United States." For the same moral cancer which Edwards had diagnosed, they prayed that God would send the healing of "true political virtue."[2]

These different resolutions of the same problem suggest in microcosm the intellectual journey of eighteenth-century New England clergymen as they attempted to resolve what it meant to be a citizen of two kingdoms, a devoted Christian and an ardent patriot. This path, spanning the expulsion of the French from America, the revolt from Britain, and the infant years of the Republic, roughly from 1740 to 1800, witnessed a profound and paradoxical change of direction, a shift of priorities easily observed but elusive to chart. During these years the clergy increasingly welcomed into the forefront of thinking a republican philosophy of history and scheme of politics that interpreted any specific political context as but another incident in the ongoing struggle between power and liberty. Yet amid this apparent drift towards a

2. *A Concert of Prayer Propounded to the Citizens of the United States of America* (Exeter, N. H., 1787), pp. 4, 9.

secular interpretation of politics, explanations of the civil order by religious symbols became even more extensive and highly charged. Far from removing political culture from the domination of religious concepts, ministers extended the canopy of religious meaning so that even the cause of liberty became sacred. The cycles of republican history and the linear perspective of Christian eschatology became indivisible, the joining of separate traditions in mutually supportive union. This study suggests that the convergence of millennial and republican thought forms a central theme in the complex relationship between religion and politics in Revolutionary New England.

This argument is rooted in the firm conviction that the current understanding of religion in the last half of the eighteenth century has fallen prey to the ever-present dangers against which Herbert Butterfield warns in *The Whig Interpretation of History*. In short, we have placed a high priority on questions framed by our own climate of opinion and neglected that which he assumes to be the first goal of the historian: to enter in some degree into minds that are unlike our own.[3] For at least three reasons conventional explanations have failed to comprehend the paradox of a republican eschatology, of growing secularity amid heightened religious consciousness.

In the first place, the modern distinction between sacred and secular has allowed the studies of religion and politics to go their separate ways in virtual isolation.[4]

3. Herbert Butterfield, *The Whig Interpretation of History* (London, 1931), p. 9.

4. Cushing Strout is a notable exception to this rule of polarity in scholarship. Appropriating Abraham Lincoln's phrase "political religion," he offers sparkling insights into the relationship of civic and spiritual concerns in American history. More particularly, he relates Puritanism, the Great Awakening, and Real Whiggery in cogent fashion. See *The New Heavens and New Earth: Political Religion in America* (New York, 1974).

Unlike the surprisingly undifferentiated thinking of two centuries ago, the scholarship of religious historians such as Alan Heimert, Sacvan Bercovitch, Sydney E. Ahlstrom, and William G. McLoughlin rarely intersects the equally significant political studies of scholars such as J. G. A. Pocock, Bernard Bailyn, Pauline Maier, and Gordon S. Wood. Students trying to come to terms with these contrasting approaches have found little common ground on which to explore what Cushing Strout calls "political religion" and thus to bring together conceptual worlds that for the Revolutionary generation never were separate. Although the study of ideology has matured tremendously in the separate spheres of politics and religion, one finds little precedent for the study of the politics of religious conviction by scholars with a firm grasp of both Anglo-American political ideology and the heritage of New England theology and historical self-consciousness.

A second impediment to entering minds unlike our own is that studies of religion and politics in Revolutionary America have focused almost exclusively on the influence of the former on the latter. From a modern point of view, of course, reasoning from religion to politics has the logical appeal of moving from the lesser to the greater. Alan Heimert and Bernard Bailyn, for example, despite conflicting interpretations, have both framed the discussion of religion and the Revolution around the question of the political import of religion.[5]

An equally important and potentially more suggestive line of inquiry is to examine the impact of war and political upheaval upon religious belief. John Shy has made the pointed reminder that the events and patterns of

5. Bernard Bailyn, "Religion and Revolution: Three Biographical Studies," in *Perspectives in American History*, 4, (1970): 85–169; Alan Heimert, *Religion and the American Mind from the Great Awakening to the Revolution* (Cambridge, Mass., 1966).

armed struggle have a dramatic impact upon the way
people think about themselves and the world in which
they live.[6] War made particularly heavy demands upon
clergymen who had to respond to ultimate questions with
answers that were plausible. In doing so, the press of
events often prompted them to move beyond conventional beliefs. It should therefore not be surprising to find
that war with France had a more lasting effect upon New
England millennial thought than did the Great Awakening; or that the most innovative theology of the future
since the Reformation emerged as Americans prepared
for war in the spring of 1776.

Thinking about religion primarily in terms of its political consequences has also meant that religious vocab-
ularics have too easily been viewed as a constant, an
idiom which at any point evidenced the vitality of Puritan
influence in a changing political world. Taken with the
majesty and power of Puritan ideas in the seventeenth
century, many scholars have emphasized the derivative
quality of Yankee religion in the eighteenth, as though the
Revolutionary era unfolded as just another chapter in an
ongoing Puritan epoch.[7] Taking a different tack, the ar-

6. John Shy, *A People Numerous and Armed: Reflections on the Military Struggle for American Independence* (New York, 1976), ix–xv.
7. Religious historians have too easily forgotten the way in which language behaves and might well take the advice of the literate Dorothy Sayers: "Words alter their meaning in course of time and in various contexts: to change the metaphor a little, they are like magnets charged with power that affect and deflect all the instruments of precision which come within their field of influence." The attempt to reduce such patterns of understanding as the jeremiad, the millennium, and the typoligical identity of New England to symbols of inflexible meaning resembles what Sayers describes as "the process of trying to force a large and obstreperous cat into a small basket. As fast as you tuck in the head, the tail comes out, when you have at length confined the hind legs, the fore paws come out and scratch; and when, after a painful struggle, you shut down the lid, the dismal wailings of the imprisoned animal suggest that some essential dignity in the creature has been violated and a wrong done to its nature." See *Unpopular Opinions* (London, 1946), pp. 43–44. For an incisive discussion of the nature of political idioms as they evolve, see J. G. A.

gument here presented suggests that traditional Puritan symbols were renewed precisely because they had undergone so much change.[8]

Our understanding of political religion has likewise been obscured for a third reason: a dualistic assumption within the minds of many religious historians that attribute religious change either to an intellectual tradition of the mind or to one of the spirit. Sidney E. Mead speaks for a whole generation of scholars when he concludes that "the two live movements in European and American Christianity during the eighteenth century were rationalism and pietism.[9] Unfortunately, this approach has limited the search for the political implications of religion to questions that can be answered in the outworking of one or the other of these theological perspectives.

"The first task, when undertaking the study of any phenomenon," suggests Dorothy Sayers, "is to observe its most obvious feature; and it is here that most students fail."[10] Historians of religion in eighteenth-century New England unfortunately swell the ranks of this majority. Preoccupied with tracing every political distinction between evangelical and rational religion, they have missed the most towering feature before them, the overwhelming

Pocock, "Languages and Their Implications: The Transformation of the Study of Political Thought," in Pocock, *Politics, Language and Time: Essays on Political Thought and History* (New York, 1971), pp. 3–41.

8. The sociologist Peter Berger has forcefully developed the idea that religious belief can actually be renewed by the apprehension of secular understanding. Religious symbols which no longer seem to ring true can regain their plausibility when translated according to secular grammers. These insights and many others related to the sociology of knowledge and the nature of secularization have been invaluable at coping with the changing implications of eighteenth-century religious language. See "A Sociological View of the Secularization of Theology," *Journal for the Scientific Study of Religion* 6 (1967): 3–16; *The Sacred Canopy: Elements of a Sociological Theory of Religion* (Garden City, N. Y., 1967); and *A Rumor of Angels: Modern Society and the Rediscovery of the Supernatural* (New York, 1969).

9. Sidney E. Mead, *The Lively Experiment: The Shaping of Religion in America* (New York, 1963), p. 38.

10. Sayers, *Unpopular Opinions*, p. 116.

political unity of the Congregational clergy. Despite on-going doctrinal debate, clergymen across the entire theological spectrum followed a singular path of political logic in espousing the cause of Britain against France, America against Britain, and Federalism against the Democratic Republicans. While historians have too read-ily assumed that the rotation of the theological world was the prime determinant of political religion, they have forgotten that clerical attitudes also revolved about the center of a much larger intellectual universe which could have altered profoundly the climate of opinion for Old and New Lights alike.

Republican values certainly colored clerical thinking without theological distinction. But equally significant are those religious perspectives held in common by New England Congregationalists despite open theological var-iance. Like Anglicans and Puritans of the preceding cen-tury, Old and New Lights challenged one another with such bitter invective because in the deepest sense each side understood the other as intellectual brothers, coheirs of a tradition that gave common definition to both the nature of the political process and the role of New England in the overall movement of history.[11] Unfortunately this singu-

---

11. In noting "the vast substratum of agreement which actually underlay the disagreement between Puritans and Anglicans," Perry Miller concludes that "if we make an exhaustive enumeration of ideas held by New England Puritans, we shall find that the vast majority of them were precisely those of their opponents." See Miller, "Introduction," in *The Puritans* ed. Miller and Thomas H. Johnson, rev. ed. (New York, 1963), 1:10, 7. A similar argument is made in Timothy Hall Breen, "The Non-Existent Controversy: Puritan and Anglican Attitudes on Work and Wealth, 1600–1640," *Church History* 36 (1967): 264. C. S. Lewis argued that it was always dangerous to underestimate the similarities of disputants: "Nothing strikes me more when I read the controversies of past ages than the fact that both sides were usually assuming without question a good deal which we should now absolutely deny. They thought that they were as completely opposed as two sides could be, but in fact they were all the time secretly united—united *with* each other and *against* earlier and later ages—by a great mass of common assumptions." Introduction to St. Athanasius' *The Incarnation of the Word of God,* trans. by a Religious of C. S. M. V. (London, 1944), p. 7.

lar vision has been artificially separated by too great an emphasis on theological distinctions.

In this perspective it is appropriate to refer to a political religion of *the* New England clergy. As characteristically united in politics as they were divided in theology, New England ministers voiced a common perspective on civil government so deep and unquestioned that it has eluded the kind of forthright definition hammered out when fiery theological issues were taking shape on the anvil of protracted debate. Rarely articulated with systematic precision, this fundamental agreement surfaced in a constellation of spontaneous images. This study is an attempt to bring to light the kind of social thought that Sidney Mead describes as "so deeply pervasive and widely accepted that it becomes a part of the common consciousness and passes into the realm of motivational myths.[12]

This is not to say that sermons in Revolutionary New England were the products of a unitary New England mind that imposed its relentless will upon any pastor who turned his thought to politics. Yet is does emphasize that, despite the complexity of local issues and divergent personalities, an ideology of surprisingly uniform dimensions emerged among the Standing Order.[13] This was sustained and reinforced, no doubt, by the stiff challenges to their position as an authoritative religious elite. In an age when Baptists and other dissenters from the right and

12. Mead, *The Lively Experiment,* p. 75.

13. In viewing ideology as a cultural system, Clifford Geertz emphasizes the intricate network of symbols which any society maintains as a background against which the flow of life can be evaluated. These cultural patterns function as "programs" to order the data of human experience. See Clifford Geertz, "Ideology as a Cultural System," in *Ideology and Discontent,* ed. David E. Apter (New York, 1964), pp. 47–76. For an equally enlightening discussion of thought as primarily a public activity, see Peter L. Berger and Thomas Luckman, *The Social Construction of Reality: A Treatise in the Sociology of Knowledge* (Garden City, N.Y., 1966).

Jeffersonians from the left denounced the privileged status of Congregational ministers, they had every social reason to downplay their theological differences and form a solid intellectual front. And while they continued intramural sparrings about theology, they projected a common vision of a Christian republic deeply rooted in the needs of their own social group. It was hardly coincidental, for instance, that clergymen identified tax support of their own profession as a cornerstone of republican stability. It is the goal of this study to unravel the systems of meaning that helped New England ministers legitimate their needs and interests in terms of their religious ideals.[14] On a certain level, ironically, the idea of a "New England mind" may be far more applicable to the embattled Standing Order of this period than to their ancestors, who found that their commanding position in society actually bred a measure of independent thought.

Two other assumptions have guided this research from the start. Because my aim has been to understand the interwoven set of values by which ministers in general ordered reality, I have given less attention to formal treatises, either political or theological. Far more instructive in deciphering the clergy's taken-for-granted assumptions has been the vast array of fast, thanksgiving, anniversary, election, militia, and week-to-week sermons that issued from printing presses throughout New England. In these less guarded commentaries on political events, clergymen were likely to express their most com-

14. I agree with George M. Frederickson that ideology properly studied mediates between social reality and abstract ideals. He defines ideology as "the set of principles, programs, and goals that reflect the way a social group applies its values and attitudes to the problems it faces at a particular time." See Frederickson's review of David Brian Davis's *The Problem of Slavery in the Age of the Revolution, 1770–1823*, a splendid model of such intellectual history (*The New York Review of Books* 22, no. 16 [October 16, 1975]: 38–40).

pelling hopes and fears. Their oblique references to Antichrist or the millennium, for example, provide a much
better gauge of social thought than works that detailed
eschatology in systematic coherence. Hence, the striking
features of New England's social values are not to be
found exclusively in Jonathan Edwards's theology of the
end times or Jonathan Mayhew's doctrine of resistance to
authority. These are but single pieces in the overall
mosaic that emerges from examining the rhetoric of
scores of ministers and hundreds of sermons. Under this
kind of analysis, a flurry of isolated, off-the-cuff, and
individually incomprehensible remarks begin to coalesce
and take shape. We are thus able to discern the ideology
by which these men characterized and legitimated their
experience.

With an approach to analyzing collective consciousness firmly in mind, I have worked from a second assumption aimed at unraveling the ideology of these men.
Following the insights of William Haller and J. G. A.
Pocock,[15] I have surveyed a given frame of reference from
the following vantage points: (1) myths that men construct about their own past and the manner in which they
are used as a focus that binds men together in crisis; (2)
projections of the future course of history that similarly
reveal the deepest aspirations and central values of society; (3) characterizations that men use to depict their
most dreaded foes, both foreign and domestic; and (4)
descriptions that are used to explain a society's role, both
civil and religious, in the unfolding drama of history. In
probing the intricate myths by which Yankees understood New England's founding, her typological relation

15. J. G. A. Pocock, *The Ancient Constitution and the Feudal Law* (Cambridge, 1957); William Haller, *The Elect Nation: The Meaning and Relevance
of Foxe's Book of Martyrs* (New York, 1963).

to Old Testament Israel, her battles with Antichrist, and her millennial future, this study concerns eschatology in the broadest sense.[16] Hope can never be divorced from memory, for the past, as Carl L. Becker observed, "is a kind of screen upon which we project our vision of the future. . . ."[17] Republican thought, accordingly, did more than reshape New England's forward vision; the same assumptions that gave a new form to the "last days" also produced a usable history, an image in keeping with the direction that new "signs of the times" revealed history to be taking.

The fresh designs that appear on the tapestry of historical awareness during the years 1740–1800 demonstrate the kind of language shift that Pocock has called a conceptual or paradigmatic revolution.[18] However imperceptibly this new intellectual constellation came into prominence, these years witnessed a fundamental reordering of values that gave a profoundly new religious significance to the function of man as citizen, to the principles governing the civil order, and to the role of nations and political kingdoms in the scheme of providential history. Far from being a process that removed the political sector from the domination of religious symbols—a plausible inference from studies that treat this period of religious history primarily in terms of the separation of church and state and the rise of religious liberty—this intellectual shift saw the expansion of New

---

16. Typology is a method of interpreting the Old Testament that relates its events and characters to Christ himself and, through him, to the history of the church. A major focus of typology among New England Puritans was to see their own society prefigured in Old Testament Israel. See *Typology and Early American Literature,* ed. Sacvan Bercovitch (Amherst, Mass., 1972).

17. Carl L. Becker, "What are Historical Facts?" *Western Political Quarterly* 8 (1955): 337.

18. Pocock, *Politics, Language and Time,* pp. 13, 277.

England's functional theology to include republican ideas as a primary article of faith.[19] The resulting creed, what might well be called a "republican eschatology," became a surprisingly stable index for interpreting politics in the last third of the century as it translated the most evocative Puritan religious forms according to the grammars of republican values. With the reconstruction of typology depicting Israel as a republic, of the jeremiad portraying early New England as a bulwark against tyranny, and of the millennium envisioning a kingdom of civil and religious liberty, the clergy appropriated the means of traditional religion to accomplish the ends of civic humanism, goals which previously had not been a theological priority.[20] This synthesis left its indelible imprint upon the Standing Order's political behavior and its spiritual understanding.

Like the medieval church, Congregational thought in the eighteenth century dominated the world of civil government but was consequently dominated by that world. In defining republican liberty as a cardinal principle of Christian belief, the New England minister had to follow

19. In his study of political theology in the late Middle Ages, Ernst H. Kantorowicz has argued that secularization occurred not primarily by a contraction of the influence of religious concepts but by their inflation in mysticizing the body politic of the realm. That such a term as *corpus mysticum* came to refer to the state was clear evidence of a trend of "borrowing from the wealth of ecclesiastical notions and of transferring to the secular commonweal some of the supernatural and transcendental values normally owned by the Church." Political religion in eighteenth-century New England functioned in a manner remarkably similar to this model, as ministers appropriated religious values, imagery, and emotional force to legitimate secular political ideals and institutions. Secularization entered in both cases by broadening the scope of what was considered to be sacred. See *The King's Two Bodies: A Study in Mediaeval Political Theology* (Princeton, N. J., 1957), pp. 207–232, quotation on p. 208.

20. The simultaneous tracing of eschatology, typology, and jeremiad has shown that each functions as a different reflection of a common frame of reference; all three dimensions manifest the same pattern of evolution in a republican direction.

the dictates of his conscience in new directions, that is, wherever liberty became threatened. That he rallied to the American Revolutionary cause as a veritable crusade did not follow directly from either the dynamic piety of the Great Awakening or the enlightened and progressive thought of rational religion. Ministers of contrasting theologies defended the Revolution with the full force of religious persuasion because certain aging religious symbols common to both were revitalized as they became infused with the potent connotations of a Real Whig or "Country" ideology. During the three decades before the Revolution the cause of God had come to include a particular definition of political liberty and thus against the repeated attacks of British tyranny religious commitment demanded specific and unequivocal political action.

However sharply historians have honed their skills in comprehending the impact of political religion in the era of the American Revolution, their understanding of the ideology of clerical politics after 1780 has become dull and rusty with neglect. Attributing the near-paranoid cries for order and stability arising from Federalist clergymen to an abandonment of libertarian principle, scholars have rarely taken seriously the arguments of ministers in the 1790s, much less considered it necessary to relate this reactionary climate of opinion to its Revolutionary counterpart two decades earlier. While the comprehension of a political context as momentous as the French Revolution unquestionably demanded a certain reformulation of categories, the most striking feature of the pulpit's turn to Federalism is its continuity with the earlier defense of liberty against British power. If New Englanders in the last decade of the century became alarmed by grim portents of civil and religious anarchy, it was because their fundamental allegiance to liberty included the assumption that a power vacuum was as sure a road to tyranny as the increase of arbitrary authority. The most convincing evidence that the era of 1789 has firm links to that of 1776 is the outcry against the danger of "left-wing tyranny" that began even before the conclusion of the American Revolution and characterized the 1780s. The grip of Britain had not been broken when New England ministers began to single out the leveler and the demagogue rather than the king and the tyrant as the greatest threat to the American republic. The storming of the Bastille did not precipitate a mood of reaction any more than the Declaration of Independence turned Americans in the direction of civil and religious liberty. In both cases, the heat of revolution refined the existing patterns of thought and fired them with a luster of authenticity.

The flowering of New England republican conviction sought to restrain the many out of power rather than the few in power because New England definitions of republican vice and virtue had been nourished in an intellectual soil rich with Puritan ideas of sin and righteousness. The traditional social assumptions of New England religion continued to shade the vocabulary of liberty. Heavy with ethical overtones, this republican "dialect" reflected perceptions of the republic as Christian commonwealth, virtue as piety and benevolence, vice as sin, and liberty as the opportunity to do what is right. These Puritan facets of Yankee republicanism failed to become of primary concern until the closing years of the Revolution not so much because positive definitions of virtue suddenly contracted but because preoccupation with external vice and oppression had given little opportunity to spell out the necessary qualifications for the truly virtuous citizen. It was only with the ending of conflict that eyes which had been fixed on the threat of foreign tyranny began to examine their neighbors and take note that not everyone who had opposed British tyranny had the moral character to erect a stable republic. In finding their countrymen to be a people more analogous to wayward Israel than to virtuous Rome, New Englanders revealed that they were anything but empty vessels into which prevailing republican concerns had been poured. Rather, their appropriation of a British pattern of opposition to the "corruption" of the eighteenth century had never been divested of certain social assumptions characteristic of New England. The authoritarian strain of republicanism that resulted gave Federalist ministers the same moral confidence and sense of historic continuity that clergymen had enjoyed during the Revolution.

In the last half of the eighteenth century New England ministers allowed their political options to be defined by others, namely statesmen who could devote their full energies to the function of civil government. To the realm of the church and religious belief, however, clergymen applied their particular expertise and spoke with the kind of authority which a Puritan minister had once exercised in church and state. It is particularly crucial, therefore, to understand the impact of political thought upon those systems of belief for which ministers were the primary architects. In this narrower world of thought the republicanism of the clergy had much broader influence and altered profoundly the legacy of religious belief passed on to nineteenth-century America.

Max Lerner has suggested perceptively that "Americans have tended to find their religious faith in various forms of belief about their own existence as a people."[21] The resiliency of such interpretations of American identity has been remarkable in view of the steadily eroding

---

21. Max Lerner, *America as a Civilization* (New York, 1957), 2:715.

foundations of those religious persuasions which first gave rise to credible notions that in America God had founded a new Israel, a people who would point the way to the millennial kingdom. That these themes sustained a definite accent of reality long after other forms of typological and prophetic interpretation of Scripture no longer seemed tenable suggests that at some point old forms were renovated and made plausible to an audience that had long since discarded Puritan assumptions. It is the argument of this study that between 1740 and 1800 a new foundation was laid for the tottering structures of Puritan collective identity, a base which would stabilize them for generations to come.

Clergymen in the era of the American and French Revolutions were able to rebuild the underpinnings of their own sense of mission and destiny through a rewriting of the history of Israel and a projection of the first substantively new eschatology since the Reformation. By reading republican liberty and political forms into the experience of the premonarchical Hebrews, Americans could affirm no less intensely that the society of which they were a part had been divinely chosen. They remained the antitype of Israel by their strenuous imitation of that civil and religious liberty for which Moses, Joshua, and Gideon had struggled. Having thus sustained religious vocabularies by a secular model of politics, New Englanders actually had more reason to affirm their collective election than at any time in their history. Whereas their forefathers had never fully obeyed the covenantal terms of pure and vital religion, these citizens of the United States had compelling evidence that the standards of republicanism emerging in America went far beyond what could be expected from men in a fallen world. Once they had redefined what were acceptable standards, these

Americans found that contemporary experience confirmed as never before their status as the "New American
Israel."

The eschatological dimension of this same shift reveals
the intellectual context in which the American republic
actually became the primary agent of redemptive history.
During their opposition to French and British tyranny,
New England ministers decided that the Pope of Rome no
longer served as the primary embodiment of Antichrist
and that Satan had redirected this evil power through
another agency, that of oppressive and arbitrary civil
governments. With faultless logic ministers concluded
from this innovative assumption that the main struggle
between good and evil had shifted to the arena of politics
and nations. Because Antichrist had altered his tactics
and sought to crush the church through civil oppression,
the forces of righteousness could not expect Christian
truth to flourish under arbitrary government. Throughout New England these conclusions about the nature of
the apocalyptic struggle instilled the belief that two revolutions were necessary to initiate the millennium, the
first a worldwide expansion of those principles of liberty
realized in America, the second a proclamation throughout the world of the pure Christianity embodied in
American churches. In this scheme the American Republic assumed "the soul of a church" not by accident but as
the direct result of those principles of republican eschatology which emerged in the years between America's
two Great Awakenings.

A final word should be said about the boundaries that
shape the methodology and scope of this study. In a day
of historical nominalism, when the local and particular
form the major building blocks in attempts to reconstruct
the past, I have attempted a much broader task: to chart

over a sixty-year period the structure of religious and political ideas among New England's Standing Order. This is a case study in how men do not think in isolation but form systems of meaning in concert with their fellows. The strength of this approach is its broad angle of vision, its ability to identify the nature and rate of change in an evolving climate of opinion. But it does not tune our ears very effectively to dissent and diversity, nor ground ideas firmly in the life experiences of people. In order to deal with these aspects of eighteenth-century religion and society, scholars must use different approaches— collective biography and studies of local congregations, for example.[22] Hopefully, the methodology of this effort will invite and lay the groundwork for others.

In a similar way, *The Sacred Cause of Liberty* hopes to stimulate interest in millennial and republican thought that lies outside its geographic and denominational focus. As a study of New England, it tries to avoid the common pitfall of treating other parts of America as cultural provinces of Boston. In the last quarter of the eighteenth century, in fact, New England culture may be more significant for its distinctive rather than its typical features. By 1800 Yankees were hardly in the mainstream of American life, but it is crucial for two reasons to study this part of the whole: to understand the distinct Federalism that set apart New England's political and religious elite during the period of America's first party

22. For a superb example of collective biography and the complementary insights that it can bring to the study of religion and the American Revolution, see Mark Allan Noll, "Church Membership and the American Revolution: An Aspect of Religion and Society in New England from the Revival to the War for Independence" (Ph.D. diss., Vanderbilt University, 1975). A study of a local congregation that is equally illuminating is Charles W. Akers's forthcoming article "Religion and the American Revolution: The Case of Samuel Cooper and the Brattle Street Church."

system; and to grasp the moral vision of the republic which they held to themselves but which their children would eventually spread across the Midwest. As a study of Congregationalists, this book has definite but limited application to other Christian traditions. While New England Baptists did share some conception of a civil millennium, their preoccupation with vital piety and the separation of church and state necessarily drove a wedge between the millennial and republican themes that the Standing Order so easily brought together. On the other hand, Presbyterians within New England were practically indistinguishable from their Congregational colleagues; south of Connecticut, many followed paths similar to the ones charted in these pages. Benjamin Rush, for instance, imagined a republican millennium that would rival that conceived by any Yankee clergymen.[23] But the last thing this author should attempt is to impose his own scheme upon the flurry of millennial notions set in motion by the birth of the Republic. If eschatology helped the Standing Order of New England cope with change, it also provided solace to Joseph Galloway, spokesman of American Loyalists, who spent his final years in England, writing several volumes of prophetic history; and to the eminent scientist Joseph Priestley, exiled from England, who spent his final years in America musing "expectant on these promised years." Even the eccentric Shaker Mother Ann Lee, who was jailed in 1780

23. See Donald J. D'Elia, *Benjamin Rush: Philosopher of the American Revolution* (Philadelphia, 1974), especially pp. 66–70. Christopher M. Beam discusses the millennial perspective of Presbyterians in "Millennialism and American Nationalism, 1740–1800," *Journal of Presbyterian History* 54 (1976): 182–199; as does Fred J. Hood in "Presbyterianism and the New American Nation, 1783–1826: A Case Study of Religion and National Life" (Ph. D. diss., Princeton University, 1968), pp. 108–159; and Glenn Miller, " 'Fashionable to Prophecy': Presbyterians, the Millennium and the Revolution," *Amerika Studien* 21 (1976): 239–60.

for opposing "the sacred cause of liberty," found herself
predicting enthusiastically that the millennium would
begin in America.[24]

24. Joseph Galloway's eschatological writings are *Brief Commentaries
Upon Such Parts of the Revelation and Other Prophecies as Immediately Refer
to the Present Times* (London, 1802); and *The Prophetic or Anticipated
History of the Church of Rome, Written and Published Six Hundred Years
Before the Rise of That Church* . . . (London, 1803). Clarke Garrett deals
extensively with Priestley's millennialism in *Respectable Folly: Millenarians
and the French Revolution* (Baltimore, 1975). For Ann Lee's teaching that the
millennium was becoming a present reality in America, see Rufus Bishop,
*Testimonies of the Life, Character, Revelations, and Doctrines of the Ever-
Blessed Mother Ann Lee* (Hancock, Mass., 1816); and Calvin Green and Seth
Wells, *A Summary View of the Millennial Church* (Albany, N. Y., 1848). That
New England ministers, a distinct and self-conscious religious elite, found
eschatological themes a plausible frame of reference demonstrates that extreme
concern about the end of time by no means has been limited to the alienated
and disinherited. An avalanche of millennial studies in the last decade make it
clear that in times of revolutionary change millennial ideologies can be usefully
appropriated by a wide spectrum of social classes and political perspectives.
For these developments, see "Historians and the Millennium," Garrett's introductory chapter in *Respectable Folly: Millenarians and the French Revolution*,
pp. 1–15; and Hillel Schwartz, "The End of the Beginning: Millenarian
Studies, 1969–1975," *Religious Studies Review* 2 no. 3 (1976): 1–15.

Chapter One

The Origins of Civil Millennialism in America: New England Clergymen, War with France, and the Revolution

When our Liberty is invaded and struck at, 'tis sufficient Reason for our making War for the Defence or Recovery of it. Liberty is one of the most sacred and inviolable Privileges Mankind enjoy; without it Life itself is insipid and many Times burdensome. For what Comfort can a Man take in Life when at the Disposal of a despotic and arbitrary Tyrant, who has no other Law but his Will? . . . I would entreat you to see to it that you engage in so noble a Cause for right Ends. Let your principal Motives be the Honor of God, & the defence of your Country. Fight for Liberty against Slavery. Endeavor to stand the Guardians of the Religion and Liberties of America; to oppose Antichrist. . . .
James Cogswell, 1757

No doubts clouded the Reverend Samuel Sherwood's assessment of the impending war between Great Britain and the American colonies. "God Almighty, with all the powers of heaven, are on our side," he declared to his Connecticut audience early in 1776. "Great numbers of angels, no doubt, are encamping round our coast, for our defence and protection. Michael stands ready, with all the artillery of heaven, to encounter the dragon, and to vanquish this black host." With a confidence almost prophetic, Sherwood announced the coming defeat of the "antichristian tyranny" which the British government represented; because the king's chief ministers had sipped the golden cup of fornication with "the old mother of harlots," they faced the imminent doom reserved for the wicked, persecuting tyrants of the earth. In building the climax of his address, which translated the conflict into a struggle of cosmic significance, Sherwood predicted that

21

the British attack on America was one "of the last efforts, and dying struggles of the man of sin." From this apocalyptic point of view America's victory would initiate Christ's millennial kingdom.[1]

Sherwood was by no means the only American minister whose millennial hopes were fired by the Revolutionary struggle. The cosmic interpretation of the conflict—God's elect versus Antichrist—appeared as a significant pattern in the intricate tapestry of ideas used by New England clergymen to explain the war's purpose. Moreover, by the time American victory seemed assured, the rhetoric of New England sermons was brimming with euphoric images of America's role in hastening the kingdom. The prospects for this blessed age had not seemed so bright since the founding of New England. "Vice and immorality shall yet here, become ... banished," proclaimed George Duffield, chaplain to the Continental Congress, "and the wilderness blossom as the rose."[2]

Certainly the most striking feature of this millennial language in the Revolutionary era is the way it adapted the framework of apocalyptic history to commonly held political ideas. Sermons during the war stressed repeatedly that American liberty was God's cause, that British tyranny was Antichrist's, and that sin was failure to fight the British. With the coming of peace many ministers envisioned Christ's thousand-year reign on earth as an extension of the civil and religious liberty established in America.[3] This amalgam of traditional

1. Samuel Sherwood, *The Church's Flight into the Wilderness: An Address on the Times* (New York, 1776), pp. 39–49, quotations on pp. 46, 15, 49. For a thorough analysis of this sermon, see Stephen J. Stein, "An Apocalyptic Rationale for the American Revolution," *Early American Literature* 9 (1975): 211–25.

2. George Duffield, *A Sermon Preached in the Third Presbyterian Church ...* (Philadelphia, 1784), p. 17.

3. For sermons that interpret the Revolution as the struggle of the elect versus Antichrist see Abraham Keteltas, *God Arising and Pleading His People's Cause ...* (Newburyport, Mass., 1777), and Samuel West, *A Sermon*

Puritan apocalyptic rhetoric and eighteenth-century political discourse I have chosen to call "civil millennialism," a term warranted by the extent to which these themes were directed by the society's political consciousness. Under the aegis of civil millennialism ministers of varying theological persuasions came to do homage at the same shrine, that of liberty, and expressed their allegiance in projections about the future which were as novel as they were pervasive.[4]

The language of civil millennialism has a strange ring to an ear accustomed to that of Puritan apocalyptic thought, but not because the political dimension of millennialism was itself a novelty. Englishmen since the Reformation had often been willing to oppose civil governments deemed to be under the control of antichristian power. They assumed that the frustration of French and Spanish hegemony abroad and Catholic political influence at home played a major role in bringing on the day when swords would be beaten into plowshares. Across the Atlantic, New Englanders for a century also had watched political developments for signs of the coming times. What *does* give civil millennialism its distinctive quality is the new configuration of civil and religious priorities in the minds of the clergy. In a subtle but

Preached before the Honorable Council . . . (Boston, 1776). For good examples of ministers whose millennial hopes were aroused by American victory see Ezra Stiles, *The United States Elevated to Glory and Honor* . . . (New Haven, Conn., 1783), and Benjamin Trumbull, *God Is to be Praised for the Glory of His Majesty* . . . (New Haven, Conn., 1784).

4. I have described this apocalyptic orientation as "civil" rather than "civic" or "political" because this was the adjective most frequently used by ministers to define those privileges of citizenship which increasingly occupied their attention. Several scholars who have written about millennial interpretations of the Revolution have recognized a fundamental change from earlier apocalyptic understanding. See Ernest Lee Tuveson, *Redeemer Nation: The Idea of America's Millennial Role* (Chicago, 1968), p. 24; John G. Buchanan, "Puritan Philosophy of History from Restoration to Revolution," *Essex Institute Historical Collections,* 104 (1968): 342–43; and J. F. Maclear, "The Republic and the Millennium," in *The Religion of the Republic,* ed. Elwyn A. Smith (Philadelphia, 1971), pp. 183–94.

profound shift in emphasis the religious values that traditionally defined the ultimate goal of apocalyptic hope—
the conversion of all nations to Christianity—became
diluted with, and often subordinate to, the commitment
to America as a new seat of liberty. Although its rhetoric
was conventional, this new form of millennialism, channeled in the direction of prevailing political values, stood
in marked contrast to traditional New England apocalyptic hopes.

Nothing makes this point clearer than the differences
between civil millennialism and the apocalyptic expectations of the Great Awakening. Jonathan Edwards may
have resembled Sherwood or Jeremy Belknap in the application of apocalyptic ideas to his own times and in his
post-millennial view of the future, but such similarities
are less significant than the fundamental contrasts between the two perspectives. The New Light confidence in
the progressive course of history was based on the spread
of vital piety; Christ's kingdom advanced toward its
completion by the effusion of God's spirit in widespread
revivals. The Revolutionary millennialist, on the other
hand, based his apocalyptic hopes on the civil and religious liberty that American victory over Britain would
insure. His vision of the future inspired him to attempt to
thwart the precipitate advance of power rather than to
advocate the conversion of sinners. Edwards saw the
Concert of Prayer as the primary institution for promoting the kingdom; praying bands of pious saints were the
avant-garde who would drive back the forces of darkness. In contrast, ministers such as Abraham Keteltas or
Samuel Langdon welcomed to the cause of God anyone
who would take up the sword against the Antichrist of
British tyranny. The spontaneous defense of liberty in
America encouraged them to interpret existing American
society as the model upon which the millennial kingdom

would be based. Inspired by the complex of ideas here called civil millennialism, New England ministers of the Revolutionary era resisted tyranny in God's name, hailed liberty as the virtue of the "New American Israel," and proclaimed that in sharing these values with all mankind America would become the principal seat of Christ's earthly rule.[5]

In view of the substantial differences between these two interpretations of prophecy it is necessary to re-examine the origins and development of civil millennialism in order to explain more adequately how it became so ingrained in the minds of New England ministers. Put another way, the intention is to rethink the assumption common in recent literature that the origins of civil millennialism can be traced directly to the piety of the Great Awakening. According to this interpretation, the revivals of the 1740s aroused a new, potent sense of American destiny—expressed by the millennialism of such New Lights as Edwards—which flowered into the intense religious patriotism of the young Republic. In his massive study of the mind of eighteenth-century New England Alan Heimert attributes the fervor of the Revolutionary clergy to an excited millennial expectancy that flowed from the Awakening.[6] Heimert recognizes certain characteristics of civil millennialism but sees them only as modifications of the dynamic postmillennialism of New Light ministers. In emphasizing the dominant imprint of the Awakening on the intellectual activity of the mid-

5. For an excellent example of the striking contrast between the millennium of Edwards and that of the Revolution cf. Edwards, *Some Thoughts Concerning the Revival of Religion in New-England* . . . , in *The Works of Jonathan Edwards*, ed. C. C. Goen (New Haven, Conn., 1972), 4:348–70, with the sermon by Ebenezer Baldwin, *The Duty of Rejoicing under Calamities and Afflictions* . . . (New York, 1776).

6. Alan Heimert, *Religion and the American Mind: From the Great Awakening to the Revolution* (Cambridge, Mass., 1966), pp. 59, 413–509.

eighteenth century, he not only dismisses the heritage of pre-Awakening Puritanism but also jumps quickly from the Awakening to the Revolution, assuming that the imperial wars of the period were "incidental, even irrelevant" to the clergy's definition of New England identity. Within this framework the ideas that developed before and after the Awakening had little bearing on the shifting patterns of religious patriotism. Edwards and his successors rekindled the torch of American mission and destiny lit by the founders of the "city upon a hill" and passed it directly to the patriots who fought for a new republic.[7] Although not all scholars would accept Heimert's stress on the New Light origins of the Revolution, few would doubt that the piety of the Awakening was the main source of the civil millennialism of the Revolutionary period.[8]

This interpretation is open to serious question. In the first place, if the roots of civil millennialism are to be found primarily in New Light enthusiasm, it is strange

7. According to Heimert, the Awakening shattered "the social assumptions inherited from the seventeenth century [and] allowed the evangelical ministry to offer the American people new commitments, political as well as ethical." After 1740 little of intellectual significance remained outside of the issues posed by the "two parties" formed in the Awakening. Ibid., pp. 14, 3. For Heimert's discussion of the insignificance of developments between the Great Awakening and the Revolution, particularly the Anglo-French wars, see Ibid., pp. 84–85.

8. A complete historiographical essay could be written to explain the current scholarly paradigm of tracing the origins of American patriotism and nationalism primarily to the Great Awakening. William G. McLoughlin argues that the Great Awakening "was really the beginning of America's identity as a nation—the starting point of the Revolution." See his essay "The Role of Religion in the Revolution: Liberty of Conscience and Cultural Cohesion in the New Nation," in *Essays on the American Revolution*, ed. Stephen G. Kurtz and James H. Hutson (Chapel Hill, N. C., 1973), p. 198. See also Sacvan Bercovitch, "Horologicals to Chronometricals: The Rhetoric of the Jeremiad," in *Literary Monographs*, ed. Eric Rothstein (Madison, Wis., 1970), 3:81; Darrett B. Rutman, ed., *The Great Awakening: Event and Exegesis* (New York, 1970), pp. 4–5, 70; Conrad Cherry, ed., *God's New Israel: Religious Interpretations of American Destiny* (Englewood Cliffs, N. J., 1971), pp. 29–30; and Cedric B. Cowing, *The Great Awakening and the American Revolution: Colonial Thought in the 18th Century* (Chicago, 1971), p. 203.

that its rhetoric was employed by Old Lights such as Belknap, Langdon, and Samuel West, as well as the rationalist John Adams. The prevalence of this way of thinking among men of contrasting theologies can hardly be explained simply by reference to the New Light intellectual tradition.[9] Secondly, while recent scholarship has focused on the exultant hopes that characterized the Awakening, it has conspicuously avoided the same careful analysis of New Light thought in the years of the revival's demise. There has been little effort to examine the influence of an increasingly secular society upon a millennial perspective derived from the Awakening. Scholars have not adequately considered the significance of the decline of apocalyptic hope in the later 1740s, when Americans concentrated on concerns other than vital religion.[10] The third and most basic flaw is the almost total neglect of the apocalyptic categories used by

9. When numerous opponents of enthusiastic religion discuss the Revolution in millennial terms, how can scholars assume that the Great Awakening was their common source? It would seem far more reasonable that a viewpoint prevalent among both Old and New Lights would have its intellectual origins in their shared heritage and experience rather than in the source of their theological division. Recent scholarship, moreover, has emphasized that the study of prophecies gave rational Christians such as Isaac Newton and Joseph Priestley an opportunity to explain the unfolding of providential designs in history. According to Clarke Garrett, Priestley's interest in the millennium was "continuing one of the most frequently elaborated lines of argument used by the 'rational Christians' in their controversies with the deists in the first decades of the eighteenth century. In order to demonstrate that reason and revelation did not conflict, these Christian apologists had persistently emphasized that prophecy was a demonstration of God's power that could be verified by human experience." See Garrett, *Respectable Folly: Millenarians and the French Revolution in France and England* (Baltimore, 1975), p. 126. Margaret Jacob discusses Newton's fascination with the end times in *The Newtonians and the English Revolution* (Ithaca, N.Y., 1976).

10. Few authors who discuss religion and its relation to the Revolution fathom the profound intellectual shift that Edmund S. Morgan has captured so poignantly in one sentence: "In 1740 America's leading intellectuals were clergymen and thought about theology; in 1790 they were statesmen and thought about politics." It is necessary to reconsider what happens to New

the clergy to explain their intense interest in the Anglo-French wars. Assuming that after the Awakening the clergy's sense of history included a moral distinction between the Old World and America—an incipient American nationalism—many scholars slight the importance of the conflict with France for New England thought. Looking only for signposts pointing in the direction of Americanization, they have made an easy detour around many issues, significantly imperial in character and scope, which profoundly influenced New England ministers in the two decades before the Stamp Act.[11]

૪

In 1742 Edwards anticipated with excitement the dawning of the millennium. In his defense of the Great Awakening, *Some Thoughts Concerning the Revival of Religion,* he suggested that this "very great and wonderful, and exceeding glorious work" surpassed any that had ever been seen in New England or in other lands. The great increase in seriousness, the new conviction of the truth of the gospel, and the unusual changes in young

---

Light millennial confidence when society at large substitutes politics for religion "as the most challenging area of human thought and endeavor." See "The American Revolution Considered as an Intellectual Movement," in *Paths of American Thought,* ed. Arthur M. Schlesinger, Jr., and Morton White (Boston, 1963), p. 11.

11. For Heimert nothing can be of real intellectual significance in eighteenth-century New England unless it encouraged Americanization. The Awakening was "in a vital respect an American declaration of independence from Europe." The "guiding light" of subsequent Calvinism was "a delight in the New World itself." Thus New Lights found little to interest them in the conflict with France because the drama of history no longer included foreign characters. *Religion and the American Mind,* pp. 14, 86–87, 98, 267–69. For a conflicting interpretation that sees New England intensely caught up in the French wars "as another battle to make the world safe for Protestantism and purified of popery," see Kerry A. Trask, "In the Pursuit of Shadows: A Study of Collective Hope and Despair in Provincial Massachusetts during the Era of the Seven Years War, 1748 to 1764" (Ph.D. diss., University of Minnesota, 1971), pp. 223–86.

people throughout New England were convincing signs that God would soon transform the world into the "Latter-day Glory." Edwards was so encouraged by the progress of piety that he announced that the millennium would probably begin in America.[12]

Edwards did not stand alone in interpreting the renewal of vital religion as a foretaste of Christ's kingdom. The *Christian History,* published by Thomas Prince and his son to propagate the Awakening, reflected widespread assurance that the kingdom was making significant advances. Typical was the report of Peter Thacher, pastor at Middleborough, Massachusetts: "I desire to rejoice to hear that the Lord Christ is carrying on his own Work with such a mighty Arm in so many Places . . . . If it be the Dawn of the glorious Gospel-Day; I trust the whole earth shall soon be filled with the Knowledge of the *Saviour.*"[13] In the summer of 1743 almost seventy New England ministers signed *The Testimony and Advice of an Assembly of Pastors,* supporting the revivals and declaring that these effusions of the Spirit confirmed the expectations "of such as are *waiting for the Kingdom of God,* and the coming on of the . . . latter Days."[14]

These New Lights saw the millennium as a culmination of processes at work in the revival. They pictured the imminent age of peace in images that expressed the realization of revival hope. It would be a time of vital religion, when holiness of life rather than empty profession would prevail. Confident that these ends would be accomplished by a "wonderful *revival and propagation* of religion," Edwards identified the Awakening as "the earnest," "the dawning," "the prelude," "the forerunner" of that bliss-

---

12. Edwards, *Some Thoughts Concerning the Revival,* pp. 343–44, 353.
13. Thomas Prince, Jr., ed., *The Christian History* (Boston, 1743–1745), pp. 11, 95.
14. Ibid., pp. 1, 158, 163–64, 182.

ful age which was swiftly approaching.[15] In the *Christian History* Daniel Putnam made the connection between vital religion and the millennium even more explicit when he encouraged his fellow clergymen to pray for revival in order that "the *Kingdoms of this World* may become the *Kingdom* of OUR BLESSED LORD AND SAVIOUR JESUS CHRIST."[16]

For Edwards the revival impulse greatly overshadowed any political means of overthrowing Antichrist and initiating the thousand years of peace. "The authority of princes" could never accomplish the goal of the Spirit, nor could political and military activities in themselves sound the knell for Satan's empire. This could only be done by "multitudes flocking to Christ."[17] Later, during the French wars, Edwards was often encouraged by God's providential defeat of the enemy, who fought on the side of Antichrist, but these defeats he interpreted as "temporal mercies," incentives to the more important works of repentance and revival. Even in the political realm Edwards's primary vision was of the day when "vital religion shall then take possession of kings' palaces and thrones; and those who are in highest advancement shall be holy men."[18]

15. Jonathan Edwards, *The Works of President Edwards,* reprint ed. (New York, 1968 [orig. publ. London, 1817]), 5:239; Edwards, *Some Thoughts Concerning the Revival,* pp. 353–58.

16. *The Christian History,* 1:182.

17. Edwards, *Works,* 5:239, 241.

18. Ibid., 2:480; 5:253. In a letter to William M'Culloch, September 23, 1747, Edwards reconfirmed his subordination of political and military affairs to the issue of vital religion: "New-England has had many other surprising deliverances from the French and Indians. . . . These deliverances are very wonderful . . . but there are no such effects of these mercies upon us that are the subjects of them, as God requires, and most justly expects. The mercies are acknowledged in words, but we are not led to repentance by them; there appears no such thing as any reformation or Revival of religion in the land." S. E. Dwight, *The Life of President Edwards . . .* (New York, 1830), pp. 243–44.

To their dismay Edwards and the other revivalists did not see their dreams fulfilled in the immediate dawning of the new age. As early as the summer of 1743 indications began to appear in the *Christian History* that all was not well with the revival. While the pastors explained with a touch of nostalgia the earlier spiritual movings in their churches, they wondered unhappily why the Spirit had withdrawn. "*Manna* grows tasteless and insipid after a Year or two's Enjoyment," one minister lamented, "and too many are for making a Captain, and returning to *Egypt*."[19] Throughout 1744 the clergy's dejection deepened. While not a single minister reported a fresh revival, many expressed anxiety at the "melancholy abatements" of divine grace. A letter signed by ten ministers in eastern Connecticut depicted the situation with imagery drawn not from the hopeful visions of the book of Revelation but from the humble prayer of Isaiah that in the midst of wrath God would remember mercy.[20] Even Edwards had to confess that "the work is put to a stop every where, and it is a day of the Enemy's triumph."[21]

If the Great Awakening was the catalyst that transformed postmillennialism into a dynamic paradigm to explain current events, what happened when the fires of the revival flickered and went out? How did the New Lights respond to the increasingly difficult problem of relating millennial hope to historical reality? By the spring of 1745 this problem had become acute. The *Christian History* collapsed early that year for at least the obvious reason that there were simply no revivals to

19. *The Christian History*, 1:259.
20. Ibid., 2:114, 168, 311–12.
21. Dwight, *Life of Edwards*, p. 212.

report. As New Englanders challenged the French at Louisbourg later that spring, their attention was further distracted from the concerns of vital piety. A new tour by George Whitefield went almost unnoticed amid the frenzied activity inspired by the "mad scheme" to seize Cape Breton Island.[22]

Several options, all rather unpleasant, faced the minister who had anticipated that the Awakening would issue directly into the millennium. The fact that the kingdom's advance was checked, at least temporarily, led to deferred hope among some and outright pessimism among others. The writings of Edwards, Aaron Burr, and Joseph Bellamy expressed three different responses to the pressing need to forge new links between an optimistic tradition of providential history and the discouraging facts of day-to-day experience in a society increasingly unsympathetic to the millennial message.

One solution was to take celebrational note of revivals wherever they might be found. The decline of piety in New England had no necessary counterpart in Europe or in other parts of the British Empire. In this context we can understand Edwards's increasing involvement in transatlantic affairs after 1745. His extensive correspondence with Scottish ministers reflected an interest in the success of awakened Protestantism that went far beyond any provincial commitment to New England or America.

22.   John E. Van de Wetering, "The *Christian History* of the Great Awakening," *Journal of Presbyterian History* 44 (1966): 129; Edwin Scott Gaustad, *The Great Awakening in New England* (New York, 1957), p. 79. William H. Kenney, III, has argued that after 1744 Whitefield was able to marshal widespread personal support only when he joined in the invective against the arbitrary power and Catholicism of France: "The uniformly feared French and Indian threat continued to be Whitefield's only avenue to his former following." See "George Whitefield and Colonial Revivalism: The Social Sources of Charismatic Authority, 1737–1770" (Ph.D. diss., University of Pennsylvania, 1966), pp. 158–205, quotation on p. 180.

Never again did he assert that America would have a special role in the coming of the millennium. Thus in his *Humble Attempt* of 1747, written in response to a proposal by Scottish ministers for extensive networks of Christians who would pray regularly for new revivals, Edwards showed no inclination to draw a moral distinction between the Old World and the New. In lamenting the spiritual decadence of the whole British Empire he manifested a pessimism about America no less pronounced than that he evinced about the British Isles.[23] On other occasions, in numerous letters to friends in Scotland, he contrasted the woeful decay of religion in America—"at present very sorrowful and dark"—with comforting evidences of divine activity elsewhere in the empire. In one of these letters he expressed the hope that recent news from Britain would excite New Englanders to seek God's face, if they were not too far "buried in ignorance, or under the power of a lethargic stupor." Edwards could no longer find signs of the coming millennium exclusively in America; the decline of experimental religion there forced him to look beyond the Atlantic to see God at work.[24]

Edwards's solution to the problem of relating history to millennial theory was at best a holding action that avoided the major question: how could one anticipate the millennium in a society unaffected by revivalism? What happened, for instance, when revival fires were extinguished not only in New England but also throughout the empire? This was the problem that Edwards's son-in-law, Aaron Burr, faced in the 1750s. Finding that both England and America were afflicted by irreligion and infidelity, and fearing the spiritual destruction of the whole

23. Edwards, *Works*, 2:476.
24. Dwight, *Life of Edwards*, pp. 262, 278, 287, 412.

British people,[25] Burr maintained Edwards's postmillennialism but shuffled his categories to develop a millennial vision that can only be called pessimistic.[26] Thus in his sermon *The Watchman's Answer*, Burr developed a view of history and the apocalypse that Edwards would hardly have recognized. According to Burr, the course of history since the Reformation had not progressed in a millennial direction. Not only had the initial break with Rome fallen far short of the hopes it had raised, but also in more recent times the night of antichristian domination had continued and even deepened. Burr climaxed this pessimistic argument by disagreeing explicitly with Edwards's interpretation of the slaying of the witnesses in Revelation II. Whereas for Edwards this worst time of persecution for the church had already taken place, Burr confessed his belief that the "sorest Calamity and Distress" were yet to come. The church should prepare itself to suffer cheerfully in an era of "Heresy and Wickedness, Tumults and Corruptions." Instead of sounding a trumpet of hope, Burr issued an exhortation to endurance; instead of projecting a vision of progress, he renewed the jeremiad theme.[27] He saw the millennium as the ultimate extrication of the church from its deadly lethargy, its "Midnight

25. Aaron Burr, *A Discourse Delivered at New-Ark* ... (New York, 1775), pp. 23, 28. In his interpretation of this sermon Heimert singles out Burr's denunciations of Great Britain as an indication of the increasing American dissatisfaction with Old World Protestantism. Apparently he overlooks the fact that Burr directed this criticism as much to America as to England. *Religion and the American Mind*, pp. 85–86.

26. James W. Davidson has made the excellent point that postmillennialism was not a constant "which affected the behavior of people in different times and situations in any consistent manner." He effectively demonstrates that a postmillennial framework did not necessarily imply belief in an imminent millennium, an unclouded optimism, or an intense activism to bring on the kingdom. "Searching for the Millennium: Problems for the 1790s and 1970s," *New England Quarterly* 45 (1972): 241–61, esp. 250–55, quotation on p. 255.

27. Aaron Burr, *The Watchman's Answer* ... (Boston, 1757), pp. 19–22, 34–40, quotations on pp. 22, 39.

Security." Like Cotton Mather, whose chiliasm envisioned no interruption of the downward course of the church until God supernaturally intervened, Burr articulated a postmillennialism in which only a cosmic reordering would defeat the evil forces rampant among men.[28]

Both Edwards and Burr related their apocalyptic hopes to the events of contemporary history. The failure of the Awakening thus left them no choice but to alter their views of the future. Edwards maintained his optimism by broadening his vision to include the empire; for Burr even that panorama failed to inspire hope. In contrast to both, another New Light leader, Joseph Bellamy, maintained his millennial expectations by disassociating the millennial future from contemporary history. He was thus able to speak optimistically of Christ's eventual kingdom without regard to its current record of success or lack thereof. His 1758 sermon The Millennium, without mentioning a single contemporary event, either religious or political, offered Christians only the timeless hope that someday Christ would prevail.[29]

28. For Cotton Mather's views on the second coming of Christ see Robert Middlekauff, The Mathers: Three Generations of Puritan Intellectuals, 1596–1728 (New York, 1971), pp. 320–49, esp. p. 335.

29. Joseph Bellamy, The Millennium, in The Great Awakening: Documents Illustrating the Crisis and Its Consequences, ed. Alan Heimert and Perry Miller (Indianapolis, Ind., 1967), pp. 609–35. In other sermons Bellamy displays the same exclusively religious and apolitical concern. See A Blow at the Root of the Refined Antinomianism of the Present Age (Boston, 1763); An Essay on the Nature and Glory of the Gospel of Jesus Christ . . . (Boston, 1763); and The Half-Way Covenant (New Haven, Conn., 1769). Even into the Revolutionary era, Bellamy's sharp distinction between the church and the world gave him cause not to identify the kingdom of God and the cause of American independence. In a letter to his son on April 3, 1775, Bellamy still kept political commitments at arm's length: "My desire and prayer to God is, that you my son Jonathan may be saved. And then, whatever happens to America or to you, this year or next, you will be happy forever." Tyron Edwards, "Memoir," in The Works of Joseph Bellamy, D. D. (Boston, 1850), 1:x1. I am grateful to Mark A. Noll for this citation and a thorough discussion of how the stringent demands of New Light piety did offer a critical vantage point which allowed some to escape the unconscious sanctifying of political values that is the major

The New Light millennial vision could never have provided the intellectual foundation for the historical optimism prevalent among ministers of the Revolutionary
era. Based on the success of awakened piety, it could not
sustain the interest of a generation whose infatuation
with revivalism faded as quickly as it had flowered. When
society ceased to march to the revival's cadence, the New
Light drummers faced the necessity of developing a more
compelling beat. The Anglo-French conflicts that claimed
New England's attention after 1745 provided just such
an opportunity. In the wars with France the New England clergy found a broader basis for a millennial hope
that could encompass all of society.

ṽ

In July 1745 the New England press reported what must
have been for its readers the most astounding news story
in memory: the French fortress of Louisbourg had been
captured by New England arms! In reactions that were
almost ecstatic, newspapers, firsthand accounts, and
sermons told how four thousand undisciplined "Land-
Men unused to War" had sailed to Cape Breton Island in
a makeshift fleet without British naval support or heavy
artillery and there had besieged and reduced the most
awesome military bastion in North America. Poetic descriptions compared the feat to the greatest victories of
Marlborough, and ministers were inspired to proclaim
that God had "triumphed gloriously over his and our
antichristian enemies." This mighty blow to the Man of

---

theme of this study. See "Church Membership and the American Revolution:
An Aspect of Religion and Society in New England from the Revival to the War
for Independence" (Ph.D. diss., Vanderbilt University, 1975), pp. 153–263.
For an example of a Presbyterian minister whose evangelical convictions
moderated his civic piety, see Noll, "Observations on the Reconciliation of
Politics and Religion in Revolutionary New Jersey: The Case of Jacob
Greene," *Journal of Presbyterian History* 54 (1976): 217–37.

Sin evoked numerous expressions of millennial hope from the clergy and pointed to the new concerns that would preoccupy them in the subsequent years of imperial war.[30]

In the years between the "crusade" against Louisbourg in 1745 and the signing of the Peace of Paris in 1763 the conflict with France gripped New England society with an overriding intensity. Villages had to be defended against unpredictable attack and forces marshaled for offensive engagements. The urgency of other public affairs faded for those who experienced the anxiety of battle, the despair of defeat, the joy of victory.[31] New Englanders in general, and clergymen in particular, perceived the "Gallic peril" as a massive, insidious threat to their religion and liberties. John Mellen warned his countrymen in 1756:

Our enemies may yet triumph over us, and the gospel taken from us, instead of being by us transmitted to other nations. It is possible, our land may be given to the beast, the inhabitants to the sword, the righteous to the fire of martyrdom, our wives to ravishment, and our sons and our daughters to death and torture![32]

Similarly, Ebenezer Pemberton declared that "the fires of *Smithfield*, which burnt with such *unrelenting* fury in the

30. Thomas Prince, *Extraordinary Events the Doings of God* . . . (Boston, 1745), p. 20; Joseph Sewall, *The Lamb Slain* . . . (Boston, 1745), p. 29. I am grateful to Professor G. A. Rawlyk for alerting me to research on the psychological impact of the Louisbourg Campaign upon New Englanders. See his own work, *Nova Scotia's Massachusetts: A Study of Massachusetts–Nova Scotia Relations, 1630–1784* (Montreal, 1973), pp. 172–79; and that of S. E. D. Shortt, "Conflict and Identity in Massachusetts: The Louisbourg Expedition of 1745," *Histoire Sociale* 5 (1972): 165–85.

31. For discussions of New England's intense involvement in the French wars see John M. Murrin, "Anglicizing an American Colony: The Transformation of Provincial Massachusetts" (Ph.D. diss., Yale University, 1966), pp. 118–19, and Trask, "In the Pursuit of Shadows," pp. 13, 223–86.

32. John Mellen, *The Duty of All to be Ready for Future Impending Events* (Boston, 1756), pp. 19–20.

days of *Queen Mary*," should remind New England of
the "*inhuman* barbarities" and the "methods of *torture
and violence*" that characterized French rule.[33] Mellen
and Pemberton joined a host of their colleagues who expressed their anxiety by picturing the grim consequences
of French victory. Images of enslavement, prisons, gal-
leys, and horrible tortures expressed the clergy's fear that
life under the yoke of France would be "lingering Death."
To French tyranny, Solomon Williams preferred that
New England be destroyed by an earthquake.[34]

The ministers' rhetoric associated France inseparably
with "the merciless Rage of *Popish* power" and evoked
images of the inquisition, the fury of Queen Mary, the
schemes of the Stuarts, and the more recent suppression
of Protestants in France. Roman Catholicism represented
for New Englanders not only their ancestors' most hated
foe but also an immediate conspiracy against the liberties
of all mankind.[35] Typical of this mood was the fear expressed by Prince that "our inveterate and *popish*
Enemies both without and within the Kingdom, are rest-
less to enslave and ruin us." If France won the struggle,
"Cruel *Papists* would quickly fill the *British Colonies,*
seize our Estates, abuse our Wives and Daughters, and
barbarously murder us; as they have done the like in
France and *Ireland*."[36]

These perceptions of an extensive French-Catholic

33. Ebenezer Pemberton, *A Sermon Delivered at the Presbyterian Church in
New-York, July 31, 1746* (New York, 1746), p. 10.

34. Gad Hitchcock, *A Sermon Preached in the 2d Precinct in Pembroke* ... (Boston, 1757), p. 19; Solomon Williams, *The Duty of Christian
Soldiers* ... (New London, Conn., 1755), pp. 33–34; Isaac Stiles, *The Character and Duty of Soldiers* ... (New Haven, Conn., 1755), p. 2.

35. William McClenachan, *The Christian Warrior* (Boston, 1745), p. 5;
Thomas More Brown, "The Image of the Beast: Anti-Papal Rhetoric in Colo-
nial America," in *Conspiracy: The Fear of Subversion in American History*, ed.
Richard O. Curry and Thomas More Brown (New York, 1972), pp. 1–20;
Sister Mary Augustina Ray, *American Opinion of Roman Catholicism in the
Eighteenth Century* (New York, 1936).

conspiracy were linked directly to an apocalyptic interpretation of history in which the French were accomplices in Satan's designs to subjugate God's elect in New England. According to John Burt, the conduct of the French "bespeaks them the Offspring of that *Scarlet Whore, that Mother of Harlots,* who is justly *the Abomination of the Earth.*"[37] In the years of the French wars the ministers' constant use of such highly charged images as "the Man of Sin," "the North American Babylon," "the Mother of Harlots," and "the Romish Antichristian Power" expressed their sense of the cosmic significance of the conflict and showed that the traditional apocalyptic view of history retained great power.[38]

In delineating this moral dichotomy between themselves and the French, New Englanders altered the patterns of apocalyptic thought. Turning from spiritual introspection, they began to underscore their collective role in the last decisive struggle with Satan. Rather than becoming "indifferent to and weary with" this interpretation of history, clergymen at mid-century manifested an intensity of interest in Antichrist's overthrow unknown since the time of John Cotton and Edward Johnson.[39]

36. Thomas Prince, *A Sermon Delivered At the South Church in Boston* . . . (Boston, 1746), pp. 12, 18.

37. John Burt, *The Mercy of God to His People* . . . (Newport, R.I., 1759), p. 4.

38. Nathaniel Appleton, *A Sermon Preached October 9* . . . (Boston, 1760), p. 36; Williams, *Duty of Christian Soldiers,* p. 26; Sewall, *The Lamb Slain,* p. 34.

39. Heimert, *Religion and the American Mind,* p. 85. For a concise discussion of New England's collective introspection in the late seventeenth and early eighteenth centuries see Perry Miller, "Errand into the Wilderness," in his *Errand into the Wilderness* (Cambridge, Mass., 1956), pp. 1–15. This literature of jeremiad stands in marked contrast to the European orientation of both New England's first settlers and that generation which after 1745 was preoccupied with imperial conflict. J. F. Maclear discusses the important role that Antichrist played in the thought of early New Englanders in "New England and the Fifth Monarchy: The Quest for the Millennium in Early American Puritanism," *William and Mary Quarterly,* 3rd. ser., 32 (1975): 223–60.

Vivid perceptions of an external foe confirmed their sense of identity as God's elect people living in the end times and linked their lives to the cosmic war between good and evil. In the minds of Old Lights images of Antichrist shifted from "enthusiasm" to the French menace, and New Lights ceased to be preoccupied with the dangers of an unconverted ministry. More concerned with the common struggle than with divisive questions relating to the spread of vital piety, the clergy found remarkable solidarity in a renewed sense of apocalyptic history.[40]

The response of New England ministers to French defeat reveals the power of this perspective. Had the clergy, burdened by the anxiety of war, used the imagery of prophetic Scripture as mere rhetoric to stir their countrymen to fight, one would expect this form of discourse to have ended with the cessation of conflict. Yet British victories, far from signaling the demise of the apocalyptic vision, gave rise to an unprecedented outpouring of hope that Christ's kingdom was imminent. When Louisbourg fell, ministers overcame their theological differences to join in a harmonious chorus of millennial rejoicing. Not only would the Man of Sin no longer rule as vice-regent in the area of Cape Breton, but the conquest of Louisbourg was a sign that the day was not far off when it would be proclaimed that "Babylon the Great is fallen."[41] Less than a year later the defeat of the Pretender at Culloden

40. The intensity of Old Light hatred of factionalism can be seen in Charles Chauncy, *Seasonable Thoughts on the State of Religion in New-England* (Boston, 1743), p. 175; and Isaac Stiles, *A Prospect of the City of Jerusalem* ... (New London, Conn., 1742), p. 45. There was remarkable unanimity, for instance, in the Old and New Light reactions to the Louisbourg campaign. Cf. the thanksgiving sermons given on the same day by Prince, *Extraordinary Events, and* Charles Chauncy, *Marvellous Things Done by the Right Hand and Holy Arm of God* ... (Boston, 1745).

41. Sewall, *The Lamb Slain*, p. 34; Chauncy, *Marvellous Things*, p. 21.

evoked even greater displays of millennial expectancy.[42] Not since the rousing times of the Awakening had the ministers been so sure that the new age was about to dawn.

For the duration of the French wars the apocalyptic dimensions of the conflict became even more pronounced in the minds of the clergy. By the mid-1750s references associating France with Antichrist had increased significantly.[43] Nor was this perspective limited to New England. For the Virginian Samuel Davies the contest of an all-Catholic French alliance with an all-Protestant British coalition suggested nothing less than "the commencement of this grand decisive conflict between the Lamb and the beast." Without qualification he pictured the consequence of French victory as the slaying of the witnesses after which Antichrist would establish his reign. French defeat, on the other hand, would introduce the most significant revolution in history, namely, *"a new heaven and a new earth."*[44]

When the long-awaited news of French downfall in Canada reached New England, millennial optimism knew no limits. In sermon after sermon ministers celebrated the removal of the last and greatest obstruction to the coming kingdom. Typical was the thanksgiving sermon of Nathaniel Appleton, who delighted in God's

42. Hull Abbot, *The Duty of God's People to Pray for the Peace of Jerusalem* . . . (Boston, 1746), pp. 25–26; Prince, *Sermon Delivered at the South Church*, p. 37.

43. Trask notes that there were more publications with eschatological themes during the 1750s than in any other decade of the colonial period. "In the Pursuit of Shadows," p. 199.

44. Davies presented this apocalyptic interpretation of the war in a fast sermon at Hanover, Virginia, in October 1756. See Samuel Davies, "The Crisis: or, the Uncertain Doom of Kingdoms at Particular Times," in his *Sermons on Important Subjects* (Philadelphia, 1818), 5:239–66, quotations on pp. 257–258.

judgment upon the French—"a Vial of his Wrath [poured] upon this Part of Antichrist"—and anticipated the "greater and more marvellous Works" that God was about to accomplish. Samuel Langdon anticipated the "final ruin of that spiritual tyranny and *mystery of iniquity.*" The time was at hand for the shout of general joy: "*Babylon the great is fallen, is fallen!*"[45] Jonathan Mayhew, reversing his pessimistic estimation of the course of history prompted by the earthquake of 1755, expressed elation that God was revealing His purpose to destroy the Beast; in confounding the antichristian forces by a succession of judgments He would initiate "a most signal revolution in the civil and religious state of things in this world; and all the kingdoms thereof are to become the kingdoms of our Lord."[46] Only such acts of divine intervention as the Reformation, the defeat of the Armada, the overthrow of the Stuarts, the founding of New England, and the accession of the Hanoverians could be compared with the conquest of Canada, a victory that Solomon Williams declared to be "of more Importance than has ever been made by the *English,* since *England* was a Nation."[47]

In light of this rhetoric the suggestion that New England ministers had disengaged from the French and Indian War or saw it as "incidental, even irrelevant, to the central theme of history" seems as unbelievable as eighteenth-century Harvard College requesting the Pope to give the Dudleian Lecture. Far from withdrawing from

45. Appleton, *Sermon Preached October 9*, pp. 1–6, 26, 36; Samuel Langdon, *Joy and Gratitude to God . . .* (Portsmouth, N.H., 1760), pp. 42–43. See also Andrew Eliot, *A Sermon Preached October 25th 1759 . . .* (Boston, 1759), p. 42.

46. Jonathan Mayhew, *Two Discourses Delivered October 25th, 1759 . . .* (Boston, 1759), pp. 49, 61.

47. Solomon Williams, *The Relations of God's People to Him . . .* (New London, Conn., 1760), p. 19. See also Thomas Barnard, *A Sermon Preached before his Excellency Francis Bernard . . .* (Boston, 1763), pp. 36–44.

the imperial conflict, New Englanders translated it into genuinely cosmic categories. Fighting the French became the cause of God; marching to battle hastened the destruction of Antichrist; victory proclaimed a "Salvation, a Deliverance, by far superior to any—nay to all that *New-England* ever experienced."[48] If there were still some clergymen who in 1760 could not discern the progress of providential history in the French defeat and who still found their spirits uplifted solely by the Concert of Prayer, they were few and insignificant. With rare exceptions the clergy saw the war's end as unequivocal evidence that the kingdom of darkness could no longer restrain the latter-day glory. "What a Scene of Wonder opens to our View!" exclaimed Mather Byles, almost breathless with anticipation. "Good God! what an astonishing Scene of Wonders! Methinks, a universal Transport animates every Countenance, and sparkles in every Eye."[49]

By 1760 New England clergymen appear to have lost a clear distinction between the kingdom of God and the goals of their own political community. Military victories of Protestants over Catholics, which for earlier New Englanders had been means to the end of worldwide revival, now pointed toward a different end. The idea of a millennium of liberty both civil and religious had captured the clergy's imagination. During the two decades of war with France ministers had continued the long-established practice of aligning their own cause with that of God, but these years had worked a reordering of the clergy's values and priorities. Yet because the French wars were not the only cause of this widespread shift, one must trace other,

---

48. Heimert, *Religion and the American Mind,* p. 85; Eli Forbes, *God the Strength and Salvation of His People . . .* (Boston, 1761), p. 9.

49. Mather Byles, *A Sermon, Delivered March 6th 1760 . . .* (New London, Conn., 1760), p. 13.

no less crucial, intellectual changes by which Antichrist became much more a symbol of tyranny than of heresy and the millennium much more an age of liberty than of piety.

꽃

Rarely did New Englanders tire of building myths about the heroic acts of the founders of "the city upon a hill." For the historian these myths are important because they reflect their authors' values and were used by them to express their concerns.[50] In analyzing the rhetoric of the jeremiad, Perry Miller has shown how second- and third-generation New England ministers reproached their contemporaries by constructing exalted myths of the early settlers. Similarly, by tracing the formulation of myths during the two decades after 1740 we can more easily grasp the changing values and interests of the eighteenth-century ministers who created them.[51]

Although the Great Awakening shattered the traditional jeremiad model, it did not replace it. Rather, it bisected the earlier myth so that each side in the dispute over enthusiastic religion inherited a part. In contrasting the example of the first generation with the declension of their own age, both Old and New Lights focused on the particular characteristics of the founders that confirmed their own points of view. While New Lights exalted the "Power of Religion among the primitive Planters" and lamented its subsequent decay, Old Lights dwelt upon the love and unity of the first settlers and bemoaned the "Unscriptural Separations and Disorderly Practices" that

50. Wesley Frank Craven, *The Legend of the Founding Fathers* (New York, 1956), pp. 1–65; Carl Bridenbaugh, *Mitre and Sceptre: Transatlantic Faiths, Ideas, Personalities, and Politics, 1689–1775* (New York, 1962), pp. 171–206.
51. Perry Miller, *The New England Mind: From Colony to Province* (Cambridge, Mass., 1953), pp. 27–39.

disturbed their own day.[52] Most important, neither of these myths about early New England differed in substance from the interpretation that characterized the traditional jeremiad. Both the New Light emphasis on vital religion and the Old Light stress on unity and charity were fragments of the same earlier myth that had honored the forefathers for both their piety and their harmony.[53]

During the French wars this religious mythology underwent a massive change. As early as 1736 Prince pointed in the new direction when he called for imitation of the "worthy Fathers" not only for their vital and pure Christianity, but also for their "LIBERTY both *Civil* and *Ecclesiastical.*"[54] Reflecting the increasing concern of New Englanders for the privileges confirmed to them by the Glorious Revolution and the Massachusetts Charter of 1691, this new emphasis began to appear in numerous sermons on the nature of good government, but it was

52. *The Christian History,* 1:37; Stiles, *Prospect of Jerusalem,* p. 46. For New Light statements that idealized the power of vital religion among the first generation see *The Christian History,* 1:1, 72, 98, 106. Old Light jeremiads, which emphasized the unity of New England's founders, are seen in William Worthington, *The Duty of Rulers and Teachers in Unitedly Leading God's People . . .* (New London, Conn., 1744), pp. 23–24, and Nathaniel Appleton, *The Great Blessing of Good Rulers . . .* (Boston, 1742), p. 42.

53. Both of these themes are evident in such earlier jeremiads as that of Samuel Danforth, *A Brief Recognition of New Englands Errand into the Wilderness* (1671), in *The Wall and the Garden: Selected Massachusetts Election Sermons 1670–1772,* ed. A. W. Plumstead (Minneapolis, Minn., 1968), pp. 65–67.

54. Thomas Prince, *A Chronological History of New England* (Boston, 1736), Vol. 1, "Dedication," p. ii. The altered myth reflects an intellectual transition over several decades that T. H. Breen describes as a "Country persuasion." During the 1720s, James Franklin's *The New England Courant* introduced Yankees to the writings of English "Country" pamphleteers. See Breen, *The Character of the Good Ruler: A Study of Puritan Political Ideas in New England, 1630–1730* (New Haven, Conn., 1970), pp. 229–87. John Bernard in 1734 became the first minister to extol mixed-government theory and the glories of the British constitution before the General Court. His election sermon is found in Plumstead, *The Wall and the Garden,* 229–87.

only after the Awakening that the myth of the forefathers as stalwarts of liberty became a dominant theme, revealing the clergy's changing concerns.

In 1754 Mayhew articulated the form of this myth, which would become standard for the following generation. "Our ancestors," he declared, "tho' not perfect and infallible in all respects, were a religious, brave and virtuous set of men, whose love of liberty, civil and religious, brought them from their native land, into the American deserts."[55] By the end of the French and Indian War this grafting of Whig political values onto the traditional conceptions of New England's collective identity was virtually complete. In his thanksgiving sermon for the victory at Quebec Samuel Cooper reflected on New England's history and surmised that his progenitors had transplanted themselves into the wilds of America because they were "smitten with a Love of Liberty, and possessed with an uncommon Reverence to the Dictates of Conscience."[56] In repeating this interpretation of the myth New England ministers did not argue for a more secular interpretation of their own origins. Instead, they incorporated certain prevailing political values into a framework that still idealized the religious motivations of their ancestors. It was not piety alone but also the sacred cause of liberty that inspired migration to the New World.[57]

The new terms of this myth indicate the evolution of the clergy's definition of their society's meaning and purpose as with greater frequency and intensity they attributed religious significance to commonly held political values. This quest for "civil and religious liberty" became the social ideal of clergymen who in many cases came

55. Jonathan Mayhew, *A Sermon Preach'd in the Audience of His Excellency William Shirley* . . . (Boston, 1754), p. 23.

56. Samuel Cooper, *A Sermon Preached before His Excellency Thomas Pownall* . . . (Boston, 1759), p. 48.

57. Eliot, *Sermon Preached October 25th*, p. 17.

close to identifying piety with Whiggery. Benjamin Stevens expressed the sentiment of a growing number of ministers when he proposed that "liberty both civil and religious is the spirit and genius of the sacred writings."[58]

This new pattern of identity found expression in distinctly apocalyptic categories. The civil and religious liberty of British Protestants became the divine standard against the antichristian foe of French popery and slavery. In a sermon to soldiers in 1757 James Cogswell indicated the civil priorities that had come to evoke a religious reaction:

I would entreat you to see to it that *you engage in so noble a Cause for right Ends*. Let your principal Motives be the Honor of God, and the Defence of your country. Fight for Liberty and against Slavery. Endeavour to stand the Guardians of the Religion and Liberties of *America;* to oppose Antichrist, and prevent the barbarous Butchering of your fellow Countrymen.

Cogswell urged the troops to be "inspired with an unconquerable Aversion to Popery and Slavery and an ardent Love to Religion and Liberty." In this new eschatology the French were identified with cosmic evil as much for their civil tyranny as for any other reason, and, as Samuel Davies admitted, "the art of War becomes a Part of our Religion."[59]

As the ministers more closely identified religion and liberty, it was not uncommon for them to attribute to Antichrist a plot between "the *scepter* and the *surplice* for enslaving both the *bodies* and *souls* of men."[60] The civil

58. Benjamin Stevens, *A Sermon Preached at Boston* . . . , *May 27, 1761* . . . (Boston, 1761), p. 8.

59. James Cogswell, *God, the Pious Soldier's Strength and Instructor* . . . (Boston, 1757), pp. 26, 11; Samuel Davies, *The Curse of Cowardice* . . . (Woodbridge, N. J., 1759), pp. 2, 304. See also John Ballantine, *The Importance of God's Presence with an Army* . . . (Boston, 1756), pp. 18–19.

60. Jonathan Mayhew to Experience Mayhew, October 1, 1747, Jonathan Mayhew Papers, Boston University Library, Boston.

dimension of Satan's designs became a major theme both in the development of myths about the past and in the depiction of the French threat. In this way New Englanders moved in the direction of equating the attacks of the Evil One with the threat of "slavery" common to Whig ideology.[61] Thus when John Adams in 1765 pictured the course of history as a progressive, if embattled, advance of civil and religious liberty against the tyranny of Antichrist represented in the canon and feudal law, he was expressing a pattern of thought that was prevalent among New England intellectuals.[62]

Perceiving that popery and slavery had struck a bargain for their destruction, New Englanders grounded their collective identity solidly in the ideals of British Protestantism and the British constitution. Far from developing in the twenty years before the Stamp Act a sense of America's moral superiority to England, the clergy identified Great Britain as the bastion of freedom and the bulwark against Antichrist. For most ministers the corollary of abhorring the superstition and idolatry of Popish religion was "Loyalty to the Crown . . . Attachment to the Protestant Succession in the illustrious House of *Hanover* . . . and . . . Establishment in Protestant Principles."[63] New Englanders had never been more proud of their birthright as British subjects because increasingly the liberties they most valued were perceived as those of freeborn Britons. By the end of the French wars the preachers often referred to God's British Israel and included Britons among God's covenanted people.[64]

61. Charles W. Akers, *Called unto Liberty: A Life of Jonathan Mayhew, 1720–1766* (Cambridge, Mass., 1964), pp. 81–97.

62. John Adams, *A Dissertation on the Canon and Feudal Law*, in *The Works of John Adams . . .* , ed. Charles Francis Adams (Boston, 1851), 3:447–52.

63. Abbot, *Duty of God's People*, pp. 17–18.

64. Thomas Foxcroft, *Grateful Reflections on the Signal Appearances of Divine Providence . . .* (Boston, 1760), pp. 10, 12; Langdon, *Joy and Gratitude*, pp. 23–24.

The clearest indication of the clergy's anglicization is the new dimension of their myth building. During the two decades after the Great Awakening they not only altered the purposes for which their ancestors settled New England but enlarged their myths to include Great Britain. It is fair to say, in fact, that during the French wars New England ministers gave far more time to creating a usable British past than to formulating myths about the New World. Tracing providential history as the continuous battle of liberty versus tyranny, they centered their attention on the British constitution—"the admiration and Envy of the World."[65] In sermon after sermon they lifted up the standard of British liberty against the aggressive tyranny of Roman Catholicism. Assuming that popery and slavery were inseparably connected, they discovered that all Britain's past evils were attributable to Catholicism and France.[66] According to Thomas Prince, King Charles I "married a *French Papist,* Sister of King *Lewis* XIII of *France,* which was the pernicious Fountain of almost all the Miseries of the *British* Nations ever since. . . ." Similarly, the arbitrary government of James II could be linked to his "popish and despotic Principles," as could the futile designs of Charles the Pretender, whose outlook was characterized by *"Popish* Tyranny, Superstition, Bigotry, and cruel Principles."[67]

Although the ministers did include the founding of New England among the great acts by which providence had secured their rights as free men, they focused their myth-making on the Glorious Revolution and the accession of the Hanoverians. It was King William, "the Deliverer of the Nation, and the Shield of its Liberty," who more than anyone else protected succeeding generations

65. Barnard, *Sermon Preached before Bernard,* p. 37.
66. Charles Chauncy, *The Counsel of Two Confederate Kings* . . . (Boston, 1746), p. 26; Foxcroft, *Grateful Reflections,* pp. 12–20.
67. Prince, *Sermon Delivered At the South Church,* pp. 8, 12.

from popish enslavement. Ministers repeatedly exalted the Glorious Revolution as the fountainhead of the privileges enjoyed by eighteenth-century Britons.[68] In similar fashion the standard myth portrayed the Hanoverians as preservers of liberty and Protestantism. According to Thomas Foxcroft, if George I had not come to the throne, events "might have involved *Britain,* and these Colonies with it, in Blood and Ruin, and might have entail'd Chains and Misery on the latest Posterity."[69] In another sermon Foxcroft summed up this myth of the British past:

Now to single out a few very memorable Times, and not go back beyond the Memory of many yet alive:—Never to be forgotten is that glorious Year 1688, signalis'd as a *Year of the Right Hand of the most High,* by that most seasonable Interposition of Divine Providence in the wonderful REVOLUTION; delivering us from the Perils we were in of *Popery* and *Slavery,* two of the most comprehensive Mischiefs, and securing to us our invaluable Laws and Liberties, the Rights of Conscience, and the Religion of Protestants.—Again, Never to be forgotten is that glorious Year 1714, signalis'd as a *Year of the Right Hand of the most High,* by the happy and most seasonable *Accession* of the illustrious House of HANOVER to the *British* throne; Preventing that imminent Danger the *Protestant Succession* (in the Fate of which all our valuable Interests must be involv'd) was in at that Juncture, when deep-laid Plots of Papal Enemies and false Brethren threatened to subvert it.[70]

This idealization of British liberty, both civil and religious, came to maturity in the 1740s and 1750s. Although the Anglo-French wars were by no means the single determinant of this development, the conflict

68. Foxcroft, *Grateful Reflections,* p. 20. See also Chauncy, *Counsel of Two Confederate Kings,* p. 26, and Barnard, *Sermon Preached before Bernard,* p. 38.
69. Foxcroft, *Grateful Reflections,* p. 23.
70. Thomas Foxcroft, *A Seasonable Memento for New Year's Day* (Boston, 1747), p. 70.

brought into the forefront of religious thinking certain Whig political ideals which since the seventeenth century had been latent in New England thought. Against the onslaught of popery and slavery the sacred cause of liberty became the banner under which New Englanders rallied. The clergy expressed this new feeling of identity in the themes that reflected their sense of the past and view of the future. Not only had the course of providential history followed the rise of liberty, but the triumph of liberty would be realized in the coming of the millennium. Just as New Lights in the 1740s had seen the past and future in terms of the concerns of vital piety, so clergymen at war with France expressed their allegiance to liberty in the framework of civil millennialism.

ℰ

Understandably exhilarated by the expulsion of France from North America, New Englanders anticipated the total destruction of the power of Antichrist. They had scarcely savored victory, however, when the grasping hand of tyranny reappeared in a new and dangerous form. What is remarkable about the ministers' response both to the Stamp Act and to the attempt to create an American bishopric is their application of the compelling ideology of civil millennialism to these unexpected challenges.[71] Although the threats now came from England,

71. In his thanksgiving sermon on the repeal of the Stamp Act Joseph Emerson viewed this taxation in the same historical framework in which New Englanders had seen the threat of French oppression. It was another in a long succession of attempts by popery and slavery to subvert liberty. The purpose of the taxation was "to support the pride and vanity of diocesan Bishops, and it may be by and by making us tributary to the See of Rome." Emerson feared that the conflict between England and the American colonies would weaken both so that the French or the House of Stuart might come to power. *A Thanksgiving Sermon, Preach'd at Pepperrell . . .* (Boston, 1766), pp. 11–21. In similar fashion William Patten suggested that the sponsors of the Stamp Act were "perhaps no enemies to France, and not very friendly to Christian

they represented a continuation of the Man of Sin's assault on liberty. Thus when Sherwood attributed the Quebec Act to "the flood of the dragon that has been poured forth . . . for the establishment of popery," or when Langdon suspected that British taxation originated in popish religion, they were speaking from the same perspective of providential history that had fired New England's opposition to French tyranny.[72] Attempting to identify the image of the beast (Rev. 13) Sherwood in the mid-1770s gave an illuminating demonstration of how civil millennialism could be mobilized against the British:

Whether that persecuting power be intended, that has in years past, been so cruelly and barbarously exercised in France, and other popish countries, against the humble followers of Christ, to the massacre and destruction of so many thousands of protestants; or whether there be a reference to the corrupt system of tyranny and oppression, that has of late been fabricated and adopted by the ministry and parliament of Great-Britain, which appears so favourable to popery and the Roman catholic interest, aiming at the extension and establishment of it, and so awfully threatens the civil and religious liberties of all sound protestants; I cannot positively determine. But since the prophesies represent this wicked scheme of antichristian tyranny, as having such an extensive and universal spread over the earth . . . it need not appear strange or shocking to us, to find that our own nation has been, in some degree, infected and corrupted therewith.[73]

Liberty," while Stephen Johnson feared the tyranny of "a corrupt, Frenchified party in the nation." *A Discourse Delivered at Halifax* . . . (Boston, 1766), p. 21. See also Stephen Johnson, *Some Important Observations* . . . (Newport, R. I., 1766), p. 15.

72. Sherwood, *The Church's Flight*, p. 33; Samuel Langdon, *Government Corrupted by Vice* (Boston, 1775), pp. 28–29. Charles W. Akers's intensive study of Samuel Cooper and the Brattle Street Church of Boston reveals that on numerous occasions during the War for Independence Cooper repeated verbatim sermons that two decades earlier had aroused his congregation against the Gallic peril. In 1777, for instance, Cooper responded to General Burgoyne's march south from Canada by pulling from his file a sermon of 1755 and merely substituting Englishmen for the French as "our Anti-Christian Enemies." I am grateful to Mr. Akers for permission to see his manuscript, "Religion and the American Revolution: The Case of Samuel Cooper and the Brattle Street Church."

The civil millennialism of the Revolutionary era, expressed by rationalists as well as pietists, grew directly out of the politicizing of Puritan millennial history in the two decades before the Stamp Act crisis. In marked contrast to the apolitical millennial hopes of Jonathan Edwards, which had been based on the success of the revival, civil millennialism advanced freedom as the cause of God, defined the primary enemy as the Antichrist of civil oppression rather than that of formal religion, traced the myths of its past through political developments rather than through the vital religion of the forefathers, and turned its vision toward the privileges of Britons rather than to a heritage exclusive to New England.

During the Revolutionary crisis, when ministers once again emphasized the moral distinction between the Old World and the New, ironically they did so because in the previous years their own identity had become shaped in the image of British culture.[74] The sacred cause of liberty of which the patriot clergy were so enamored was not the flowering of an incipient American nationalism planted by the Awakening, nor did the initial volley of American muskets transform the millennialism of Edwards into that of Sherwood or Langdon. Instead, the religious patriotism that animated the Revolution had intellectual roots that were far more British than American. In the early 1770s, however, the intellectual and emotional force of civil millennialism, incorporating Whig political values, was brought to bear against England itself, as ministers linked apocalyptic vision to the cause of American liberty, identified the "fixed plan to enslave the colonies" with Satan's continuing conspiracy against God's people, and detected in the growth of arbitrary power, the corruption of placemen, and the ominous threat of

73. Sherwood, *The Church's Flight*, pp. 14–15.
74. For a full description of the British orientation of eighteenth-century American culture see Murrin, "Anglicizing an American Colony."

standing armies the unabated malice of the Man of Sin. It was this redefinition of the terms of providential history that constituted the distinctive contribution of the New England clergy to Revolutionary ideology. In picturing the struggle of liberty versus tyranny as nothing less than the conflict between heaven and hell, the clergy found their political commitments energized with the force of a divine imperative and their political goals translated into the very principles which would initiate the kingdom of God on earth.

Chapter Two

Robinocracy and the Great Whore of Babylon: The New England Clergy in Revolt

... I have assumed the text only as introductory to a discussion of the political welfare of God's American Israel ... where we have realized the capital ideas of Harrington's Oceana.

Ezra Stiles, 1783

It is hardly surprising that the outbreak of the American Revolution provoked a flurry of millennial speculation. Faced with the unnerving reality of war, patriot ministers plumbed the depths of their vocabulary, seeking words to sanction the cause they espoused and to provide purpose to the destructive scenes they were called upon to witness. In the spring of 1776, for example, Samuel West of Dartmouth, Massachusetts, a chaplain in the American army, found himself so enraged by the violence of the British army, "a piece of barbarity unknown to Turks and Mohammaden infidels," that he could only describe it as the "horrible wild beast" of the book of Revelation. Depicting a seven-headed and ten-horned creature emerging from the bottomless pit, West became the first clergyman in Massachusetts history to anchor the annual election sermon in an explicitly apocalyptic text. He was so caught up by the moment, in fact, that he bent the pliable idioms of eschatology even beyond their normal limits of tolerance: "We must beat our plowshares into swords," he thundered, "and our pruning-hooks into spears."[1]

But the crucible of revolution brought more than visions of the end times into West's excited mind. It also steeled

---

1. Samuel West, *A Sermon Preached before the Honorable Council* ... (Boston, 1776), pp. 58–63.

his will for present action: to defend at all costs the cause of
liberty against "intolerable tyranny and oppression." The
experience of the last decade had convinced West and his
colleagues that appeasement and concession were the worst
possible alternatives in the growing crisis of British
authority.

It would be suicidal, they reasoned, to submit to "the
first openings of a plan to enslave the whole nation." That
they perceived a "hidden intent," a "pernicious scheme,"
a "settled fix'd plan"[2] behind the more obvious issues of
Anglo-American political disagreement suggests the particular configuration of ideas through which they viewed
the world of the Stamp Act, the Boston Tea Party, the
presence of a standing army in Boston, and the vicis-
situdes of war itself. For the clergy of New England, as for
their lay contemporaries, the clouds of war threatened "a
dreadful desolating tempest of oppression, bondage, and
ignominious servitude." "Is it merely then to impoverish
us that we are to be thus fleec'd to the skin?" asked
Samuel Webster in 1774. "No! the plot is deep, and
worse is yet behind." Sermon after sermon expressed
grave concern that the frail blessing of liberty would soon
be consumed by "the all-devouring jaws of tyrannic
will."[3] Having failed to corrupt American virtue with a
throng of pensioners and placemen, the faction at the
helm of British government imposed upon the colonies
the bane of any free people, a standing army. When even

2. Joseph Emerson, A Thanksgiving Sermon Preached at Pepper-
rell . . . (Boston, 1766), p. 13; Henry Cumings, A Thanksgiving Sermon
Preached at Billerica . . . (Boston, 1767), p. 19; Samuel Sherwood, A Sermon
Containing Scriptural Instructions to Civil Rulers . . . (New Haven, Conn.,
1774), pp. 67–68.
    3. Cumings, A Thanksgiving Sermon, p. 21; Samuel Webster, The Misery
and Duty of an Oppress'd and Enslaved People . . . (Boston, 1774), p. 24;
Stephen Johnson, Some Important Observations, Occasioned by . . . the
Publick Fast . . . (Newport, R. I., 1766), p. 11.

that failed to achieve their dark designs, the administration threw off the mask of liberty and with the iron fist of arbitrary decree plunged the colonies into civil war.[4]

The fact that clergymen in Revolutionary New England came to understand the Anglo-American conflict in terms similar to those of other less religious pamphleteers and orators should come as no surprise to students of colonial politics. Within the last decade the restructuring of the historian's comprehension of Revolutionary ideology in terms variously described as "Country," Commonwealth, opposition, Real Whig, and republican quite naturally reopens the question of clerical perceptions of the conflict. It certainly makes it unlikely that ministers were somehow deaf to this dominant language of civic humanism.[5] What does present a surprise, however, is the vitality of other vocabularies in their thinking. The intensity with which clergymen renewed an apocalyptic interpretation of their own destiny, reconstructed the jeremiad, and revived their collective sense of election

4. James Lovell, *An Oration Delivered April 2d, 1771* . . . (Boston, 1771), pp. 7–8; William Gordon, *A Discourse Preached in the Morning of December 15th, 1774* (Boston, 1775), p. 11; Samuel Sherwood, *The Church's Flight into the Wilderness: An Address on the Times* (New York, 1776), pp. 36–47.

5. For a thorough discussion of these developments, see Robert E. Shalhope, "Toward a Republican Synthesis: The Emergence of an Understanding of Republicanism in American Historiography," *William and Mary Quarterly,* 3d Ser., 29 (1972): 49–80. The most seminal works are J. G. A. Pocock, "Machiavelli, Harrington, and English Political Ideologies in the Eighteenth Century," *William and Mary Quarterly,* 3d Ser., 22 (1965): 549–83; Pocock, *The Machiavellian Moment: Florentine Political Thought and the Atlantic Republican Tradition* (Princeton, N.J., 1975), pp. 506–52; Bernard Bailyn, *The Ideological Origins of the American Revolution* (Cambridge, Mass., 1967); Pauline Maier, *From Resistance to Revolution: Colonial Radicals and the Development of American Opposition to Britain, 1765–1776* (New York, 1963); and Gordon S. Wood, *The Creation of the American Republic, 1776–1789* (Chapel Hill, N.C., 1969). In light of these works, the conclusions of Alice M. Baldwin, *The New England Clergy and the American Revolution* (Durham, N.C., 1928), which point to *Locke et praeterea nihil,* need considerable revision.

appears to the historian somehow out of step with themes such as civic corruption, the danger of standing armies, and the preeminence of civil liberty.

Recent scholarship, unfortunately, has done little to bring together in modern reflection two conceptual worlds that for Revolutionary clergymen were never separate. Despite creative new strides in the analysis of ideology in this era, most studies have developed along two paths which rarely intersect. While one perspective has concentrated on the ideology of distinctly political media of communication, the other has focused on the clergy and religious idioms. What has not yet been adequately explained is how men voiced assumptions that were both eschatological and libertarian.[6]

It is therefore necessary to reconstruct the framework in which New England ministers perceived the Revolutionary crisis in order to understand how in one breath a minister could project the rhetoric of "Antichrist" and in the next that of "Robinocracy."[7] This "conflation of the Biblical and secular historical worlds" had its inception in the political religion formulated dur-

6. The religious strain of scholarship is best represented by Perry Miller, "From the Covenant to the Revival," in *The Shaping of American Religion,* ed. J. W. Smith and A. L. Jamison (Princeton, N.J., 1961), pp. 322–68; Alan Heimert, *Religion and the American Mind: From the Great Awakening to the Revolution* (Cambridge, Mass., 1966); and Cedric B. Cowing, *The Great Awakening and the American Revolution: Colonial Thought in the 18th Century* (Chicago, 1971). The most recent example of this parochial vision is the otherwise brilliant work of Sacvan Bercovitch, *The Puritan Origins of the American Self* (New Haven, Conn., 1975). Without a single reference to "republican" scholarship and its weighty contribution to eighteenth-century American intellectual history, Bercovitch has attempted to trace from the Puritans to the Romantics "the rhetoric of American identity." Limiting his analysis to Puritan rhetoric, he finds, not surprisingly, that its imaginative power is paramount in Revolutionary America.

7. Lord Bolingbroke coined the term "Robinocracy" to describe the administration of Robert Walpole, a form of government, he explained, "in which the chief minister maintained the facade of constitutional procedures while he in fact monopolized the whole of government power." See Bailyn, *The Ideological Origins of the American Revolution,* pp. 49–50.

ing the Anglo-French wars, as reactions to British tyranny mobilized the intellectual reserve of civil millennialism against a new and more dangerous encroachment of power. Yet the dialectic of an intensified providential vocabulary and a full-blown republican ideology that emerged when the older rhetoric was applied to the awesome power of Britain poses a new and more elusive challenge to the historian. By recharting a path through the myths and images used by clergymen to order their existence, this analysis will attempt to clarify a pattern of thought that blended republican ideology and traditional Puritan forms.[8] What did Samuel West mean when he exhorted the assembled magistrates of Massachusetts to "strive to get victory over the beast and his image, over every species of tyranny"?[9]

Amid the shifting intellectual currents of eighteenth-century New England, one theme above all others maintained its hold on the clergy. It was the solid conviction that their own community had been chosen as a special people of God. Although the limits of that community did vary over time and according to the particular context of

8. The most helpful work in this regard has been Bernard Bailyn, "Religion and Revolution: Three Biographical Studies," in *Perspectives in American History* 4 (1970): 85–169, particularly p. 135. The transparent connection that is easily made between the republicanism of the English Civil War and that of the American Revolution is complicated by at least two factors. First, the early settlers of New England did not pattern their biblical commonwealths after Milton, Sidney, Harrington, or Locke. For several generations Calvinists in New England rejected the libertarian directions of English Dissent and did not warm up to the Commonwealth tradition until well into the eighteenth century. Secondly, the legacy even then was not a direct one. Yankees became enamored of Commonwealth ideas indirectly, by appropriating for their own needs the ideas of radical Whigs in England who had absorbed the seventeenth-century tradition and recast it to deal with the political and financial innovations of the Age of Walpole. The introduction of Real Whig ideology into America through men such as James Burgh and Thomas Hollis and its relation to traditional New England values are serious problems that cannot be dismissed merely by saying that Yankees somehow became champions of "the Good Old Cause."

9. West, *A Sermon Preached before the Honorable Council*, p. 67.

a given sermon,[10] the ministers' confidence remained unshaken that in some way they were to play a special role in the scheme of providential history. Confirmed by myths that God had "planted a vine in this American wilderness" which he would "never suffer to be plucked up, or destroyed,"[11] and by visions of their own special place in a millennial kingdom, this sense of identity found its deepest support in the analogy between their own community and Old Testament Israel. The assumption of the direct parallel between Israel and themselves ran so deep that few ministers of the hundreds who chose an Old Testament text and applied it directly to New England or to the American colonies bothered to make explicit the typology which Cyprian Strong explained to the people of Chatham, Connecticut, in 1777:

There is no one (I trust) whose mind is not at once struck with the description of Israel, as being a most perfect resemblance of these American Colonies: almost as much so, as if spoken with a primary reference to them.[12]

The rending of deep ties between the American colonies and Great Britain forced New Englanders to cling more firmly to traditional patterns of self-identity. Most commonly, the pulpit responded to the events of the Revolution by drawing the analogy between America and ancient Israel and by linking their own cause to that of New England's founders.[13] In more graphic expressions, however, ministers depicted the patriot standard as:

---

10. Judith A. Wilson, "My Country is My Colony: A Study in Anglo-American Patriotism, 1739–1760," *The Historian* 30 (1968): 333–49.

11. Samuel West, *A Sermon Preached before the Honorable Council* . . . (Boston, 1776), p. 56.

12. Cyprian Strong, *God's Care of the New-England Colonies* (Hartford, 1777), p. 5.

13. Ibid., p. 6; Gad Hitchcock, *A Sermon Preached at Plymouth December 22d, 1774* (Boston, 1775), p. 17.

the cause of truth, against error and falsehood; the cause of righteousness against iniquity; the cause of the oppressed against the oppressor; the cause of pure and undefiled religion, against bigotry, superstition, and human inventions. . . . In short, it is the cause of heaven against hell—of the kind Parent of the universe, against the prince of darkness, and the destroyer of the human race.[14]

With connotations even more evocative, numerous clergymen used the vivid imagery of the book of Revelation to define their own moral character vis-à-vis that of the British. The most common image of America, the fragile woman in the wilderness beset by the "malignant rages" of the red dragon, indicates that categories of Puritan providential history had not merely been reduced to "an overture to a stereotyped pattern."[15] Instead, the Revolutionary decade produced as intense a biblical description of New England as any used since the original settlement of Massachusetts.

Yet the clergy's use of the Bible remained anything but static. The novel slant of sermon texts and Biblical themes in the years after the Stamp Act gives remarkable insight into the issues most basic to the clergy's religious and political understanding. Selecting texts such as Galatians 5:1—"Stand fast in the liberty wherewith Christ has made you free"—and II Peter 2:19—"While they promise them liberty, they themselves are servants of

---

14. Abraham Keteltas, *God Arising and Pleading His People's Cause* . . . (Newburyport, Mass., 1777), 30. Keteltas had good cause to thunder against the British. A Yale graduate of 1752, son-in-law of the prestigious William Smith, and pastor of several Reformed Congregations in New York City, he was serving as chairman of a committee of correspondence when the British victory at Long Island (August 27, 1776) forced him to flee to New England. There he became pulpit supply of the Presbyterian Church in Newburyport, Massachusetts, and later of the Congregational Church in New Fairfield, Connecticut. See Franklin Bowditch Dexter, *Biographical Sketches of the Graduates of Yale College*, 6 vols. (New York, 1885–1912), 2:289–91.

15. A. W. Plumstead, ed., *The Wall and the Garden: Selected Massachusetts Election Sermons, 1670–1775* (Minneapolis, Minn., 1968), p. 354.

corruption"—ministers revealed a mental fixation on themes of liberty and slavery, freedom and bondage. The Old Testament characters of Pharaoh, the tyrant, and Nehemiah, the deliverer of Israel from captive slavery, took on new animation in New England sermons.[16] Furthermore, even when the clergy turned from pressing political issues to address the spiritual needs of their congregations, they could not escape the theme of liberty. "By nature we are slaves, slaves to sin, slaves to satan," said Joseph Emerson, "but Christ has purchased a freedom from the power of sin . . . and an eternal liberty for you in his heavenly Kingdom."[17] While one might expect such words from Emerson, who could remember his five months as chaplain on the Louisbourg venture, even New Divinity men proclaimed that the Christian gospel was "principally taken up in describing that glorious liberty which is purchased for sinners by the Son of God." Christ came to earth to

destroy the tyranny of sin and satan, assert and maintain the equal government of his Father, redeem the guilty slaves from their more than Egyptian bondage, and cause the oppressed to go free.[18]

Whereas in early New England images from the Bible were employed to define the state, apparently by 1775 political metaphors were used to explain Christianity.

The dominant role which a model of politics had come to play for all of thought is also indicated by the ultimate

16. These themes resounded from enlightened pulpits such as that of Roxbury's Amos Adams, *Religious Liberty an Invaluable Blessing* . . . (Boston, 1768); and Jonathan Mayhew's successor at the West Church of Boston, Simeon Howard, *A Sermon Preached to the Ancient and Honorable Artillery-Company* . . . (Boston, 1773). They are no less evident, however, in devoted New Lights like Joseph Bellamy's son-in-law Levi Hart, *Liberty Described and Recommended* (Hartford, 1775).

17. Emerson, *A Thanksgiving Sermon*, pp. 33–34.

18. Hart, *Liberty Described and Recommended*, p. 8; Adams, *Religious Liberty*, p. 7.

priority given to civil liberty. Gad Hitchcock explained that if men have liberty, they are:

capable of persuasion, of being actuated by motives, and by those influences from on high . . . and of being led to acquire, and support the character of religion and virtue. . . . But deprived of liberty, oppressed, and enslaved, men not only sink below the primitive standard of humanity. . . . They become stupid, and debased in spirit, indolent and groveling, indifferent to all valuable improvement, and hardly capable of any.[19]

With rather surprising logic, sermons during the Revolution expressed considerable fear that New England Protestantism would never survive British victory. They reasoned that liberty was the sine qua non of true religion, that when "earth and hell conspire against the former", they could do nothing else but "stab the latter through the side." The withering of liberty would kill off the fruit of true religion.[20]

It thus becomes evident that, despite the renewed use of providential vocabularies, the real center of New England's intellectual universe had become the ideals of liberty defined by the eighteenth-century Real Whig tradition.[21] As the Revolution intensified religious images, it also endowed them with new political connotations. That the basic structures of this universe evolved during the Anglo-French wars before 1760 does not alter the fact

19. Hitchcock, *A Sermon Preached at Plymouth*, p. 17.
20. John Murray, *Nehemiah, or the Struggle for Liberty Never in Vain* (Newburyport, Mass., 1779), p. 21; Benjamin Throop, *A Thanksgiving Sermon upon the Occasion of the Glorious News of the Repeal of the Stamp Act . . .* (New London, Conn., 1766), p. 12; William Patten, *A Discourse Delivered at Hallifax . . .* (Boston, 1766), p. 6. In his first announcement that he was siding with the colonies against Britain, Princeton's President John Witherspoon followed similar logic: "There is not a single instance in history in which civil liberty was lost and religious liberty preserved entirely. If therefore we yield up our temporal property, we at the same time deliver the conscience into bondage" (*The Dominion of Providence* [Philadelphia, 1776], pp.40–41).
21. Bailyn, "Religion and Revolution: Three Biographical Studies," pp. 134–38.

that the Revolution had a consolidating impact. Recognizing an attack against liberty far more insidious than even the schemes of the French, patriots no longer had any doubts that "the cause of liberty, united with that of truth and righteousness, is the cause of God."[22] In a collage of images which firmly established that liberty was "the fundamental principle" of the New England establishment, ministers depicted slavery as the "deformed child of Satan," espoused liberty as the "daughter of God, and excepting his Son, the first born of heaven," maintained that God's greatest judgments were reserved for tyrants, and pictured heaven as joyously awaiting those who lost their lives in the cause of freedom.[23] From this perspective it was unthinkable that a Christian would be an enemy to civil liberty. As New England marshaled its defense against the British, the clergy's confidence in divine assistance rested on the assumption that "God hath always owned the cause of liberty in North America." They could agree heartily with the firebrand physician Joseph Warren that

> if you really prefer the lonely cottage (whilst blest with liberty)
> to guilded palaces surrounded with the ensigns of slavery, . . .
> you must have the strongest confidence that THE SAME
> ALMIGHTY BEING who protected your pious and venerable
> fore-fathers . . . will still be mindful of you their offspring.[24]

That God had championed the cause of liberty by no means implied that it was proceeding, like the church,

---

22. Keteltas, *God Arising and Pleading*, p. 20.

23. Adams, *Religious Liberty*, p. 39; Johnson, *Some Important Observations*, p. 12; Jonathan Mayhew, *The Snare Broken* . . . (Boston, 1766), pp. 35, 36; Charles Turner, *A Sermon, Preached at Plymouth, Dec. 22d, 1773* (Boston, 1774), p. 48.

24. Judah Champion, *A Brief View of the Distresses, Hardships and Dangers, Our Ancestors Encounter'd in Settling New England* . . . (Hartford, 1770), p. 29; Joseph Warren, *An Oration, Delivered March 5th, 1772* . . . (Boston, 1772), p. 18.

triumphantly against the gates of hell. The pulpit's description of liberty, colored by the darker hues of opposition ideology, suggested that the tender plant of freedom was threatened with extinction. Having been driven from most regions of the globe by the encroachments of arbitrary power, liberty now found herself struggling to maintain a tenuous position even in her natural home, the British Empire. "But in what does the British nation now glory?" asked the President of Harvard in 1775. His answer summed up the general feeling that the pillars of the state had begun to tremble:

In a mere shadow of its ancient political system?—in titles of dignity without virtue?—in vast public treasures continually lavished in corruption, till every fund is exhausted, not withstanding the mighty streams perpetually flowing in?——in the many artifices to stretch the prerogatives of the crown beyond its constitutional bounds, and make the king an absolute monarch, while the people are deluded with a mere phantom of liberty?[25]

The New England clergy reasoned that the final deterrent to tyranny in Britain, the balanced constitution, now lay shattered, impotent to control the accelerating forces of arbitrary power.[26] They could interpret the unleashing of repeated attacks upon the colonies as nothing other than a direct outgrowth of this encroaching tyranny; and thus the conflict represented the defense of all that was valuable against a faction of wicked men "whose noblest plan is to subjugate the Colonies first, and then the whole nation to their will." In addition to the obvious responsibility of taking up arms as free men—"the true strength and safety of every commonwealth"—New Englanders knew that liberty would never be preserved apart from

<hr />

25. Samuel Langdon, *Government Corrupted by Vice, and Recovered by Righteousness* (Watertown, Mass., 1775), p. 16.
26. Ibid., p. 17; Cumings, *A Thanksgiving Sermon*, p. 17; Peter Thacher, *An Oration Delivered at Watertown . . .* (Boston, 1776), pp. 7–8.

a determined vigilance and a renewed spirit of civic virtue.[27]

Although Samuel Sherwood in 1774 warned his congregation in Fairfield, Connecticut, that the mischievous operations against the colonies were as black as the Gun Powder Plot, he also encouraged them that "No free state was ever yet enslaved and brought into bondage, where the people were incessantly vigilant and watchful."[28] The only hope for the success of American freedom was instantly to take alarm at the first sign that power was making an advance. Ebenezer Baldwin appealed to his audience in nearby New Haven with the same urgency: "Were a house on fire and the family securely sleeping," would it not be the height of folly to fail to sound the alarm? The visibility of luxury, bribery, vice, and oppression abroad and the confrontation at home with mercenary soldiers who "plundered and massacred" made it the patriot's primary duty to guard liberty "with a wakeful attention. . . . After a while it will be too late."[29]

In a real sense the patriots' expectations depended upon the simple maxim that the collective whole was no greater than the sum of its parts. A government, in other words, reflected the degree of civic virtue prevalent in the group of people that comprised the state. Liberty had never been externally imposed, but always sprang from a spirit that prompted men to act for the public good rather than for their own.[30] Thus, it generally followed that a people were governed in a manner which they deserved. A determined people could not easily be deceived or conquered. According to Phillips Payson of Chelsea, whose own determination led him to mount a personal attack upon the British retreating from Concord, it was

27. Langdon, *Government Corrupted*, p. 7; Lovell, *An Oration Delivered April 2d, 1771*, p. 8.
28. Sherwood, *A Sermon Containing Scriptural Instructions*, p. vi.
29. Ibid., preface to appendix, p. xlxi; Mayhew, *The Snare Broken*, p. 34.
30. Warren, *An Oration, Delivered March 5th, 1772*, p. 16.

this love of country, this public virtue, which in the
ancient Roman Republic

> was the life and soul of the State which raised it to all its glory, being
> always awake to the public defense and good: And in every state it
> must under Providence, be the support of government, the guardian of
> liberty, or no human wisdom or policy can support and preserve them.
> Civil Society cannot be maintained without justice, benevolence and
> the social virtues.[31]

This tie between individual virtue and the health of the
state led clergymen to find serious moral decay behind the
demise of liberty in Britain. If the balanced constitution
now lay in ruins and the prevalence of vice had changed
the whole face of British government, the true cause
resided in a national mood of greed and self-interest. It
was a society of corrupt persons that would subscribe to
Walpolean principles such as "everyman has his price"
and "the wealth of a people is their truest honor."[32]

The clergy of New England consistently pictured the
thirst for material possessions as the direct antithesis of
civic virtue. Nothing signaled the demise of a spirit of
liberty more clearly than men who "regarded the perqui-
sites more than the duties of office" and generally aimed
at "profitable places and pensions." One could never find
"the marks of public virtue . . . in a man who has no idea
of glory and excellency, but what he hoards up in his
barns or ties up in his purse."[33] In the minds of the clergy,
this urge for accumulation was a central motivating principle behind such specific threats to liberty as political
corruption, standing armies, the declining number of

31. Ibid., p. 16. The account of how Payson at the head of a group of
parishioners "attacked a party of twelve soldiers carrying stores to the retreating troops" is found in William Gordon, *History of the Rise . . . of the United
States* (London, 1788), 1: 483.
32. Ibid., p. 17; Langdon, *Government Corrupted*, pp. 11–14.
33. Langdon, *Government Corrupted*, p. 13; Payson, *A Sermon Preached
before the Honorable Council*, p. 14.

freeholders, and growing ignorance. They found it self-evident that "crafty ambitious men, whose only care would be to aggrandize and enrich themselves" would poison the morals of a whole community with the base arts of bribery and corruption. Likewise, they looked beyond their own experience of watching armies raise money to consider the more basic danger that money would raise an army.[34] The same crafty and ambitious men who would dismantle the constitution and maintain arbitrary power with mercenary troops would also break down the general distribution of property, thus destroying the basis of representative government and pressing a great part of the people into poverty and ignorance.[35] Becoming callous and insensitive to "the friendly instruction and warnings of the patriots' pen," men would become "the most ignorant, stupid and abject creatures in the world, fit only for slaves to domineering masters." Worst of all, there would be no recourse for men in this servile condition, as it would "always be as easy to rob an ignorant people of their liberty, as to pick the pockets of a blind man." Defrauded of their last mite of virtue, these poor creatures would join the other "nine-tenths of mankind" who languished in slavery.[36]

Although ministers became immersed in this style of opposition rhetoric, they by no means neglected traditional Puritan forms of expression. That they could speak of "God's American Israel" as a facsimile of "Har-

34. Andrew Eliot, A Sermon Preached Before His Excellency Francis Bernard . . . (Boston, 1765), p. 37; Payson, A Sermon Preached before the Honorable Council, p. 17; John Lathrop, A Sermon Preached to the Ancient and Honorable Artillery-Company . . . (Boston, 1774), p. 37.

35. Payson, A Sermon Preached before the Honorable Council, pp. 20, 21; Turner, A Sermon, Preached at Plymouth, pp. 40–41.

36. Turner, A Sermon, Preached at Plymouth, p. 40; Lathrop, A Sermon to the Ancient and Honorable Artillery-Company, p. 28; Payson, A Sermon Preached before the Honorable Council, p. 12; Eliot, A Sermon Preached before His Excellency Francis Bernard, p. 50.

rington's Oceana," Israel as a republic corrupted by
placemen, and the Earl of Bute as "an emblem of the
primitive Aaron, leading the people into all manner of
corruption" indicates the tightly woven fabric of ideas
formed by these Puritan and republican strands.[37] Ministers found it easy to define history as the cause of liberty
against arbitrary power and the cause of heaven against
hell; they bemoaned the lack of virtue and the decline of
religion; they took up arms against a standing army and
the whore of Babylon; and they anticipated the millennium and a golden age of liberty.[38]

What shatters a simplistic analysis of this kind of assimilation is a pattern of coordinate extremes. With remarkable consistency, those clergymen most prone to
apocalyptic interpretations expressed the most fear that
grandiose plots were afoot against the ancient constitution. Those who most vigorously recounted their
forefathers' errand into the wilderness argued most emphatically for the civic virtues of republicanism.[39] This
trend demonstrates that new political idioms did not
merely replace providential themes; nor were they a
parallel but unrelated influence. Yet how does one explain the vitality of Puritan forms for men who had come
to explain the crisis at hand in republican terms?

The obvious paradox of this intellectual context is that
political theories imported from England during the
eighteenth century actually sustained and renewed Puritan themes. Instead of blunting or replacing them, the
rhetoric of opposition to "corruption" in British politics

37. Ezra Stiles, *The United States Elevated to Glory and Honor* (New
Haven, Conn., 1783), pp. 7–8; Benjamin Church, *Liberty and Property Vindi-
cated...* (Hartford, 1765), p. 6; Langdon, *Government Corrupted*, pp. 11–16.
38. Keteltas, *God Arising and Pleading*, pp. 20–32.
39. Although there are definite exceptions to this pattern, it can be traced
clearly in the sermons of Samuel Sherwood, Samuel West, Gad Hitchcock, Ezra
Stiles, Abraham Keteltas, Ebenezer Baldwin, and Charles Turner.

became the essential grammar through which these earlier forms were translated in a manner plausible to eighteenth-century Anglo-Americans.[40] In the 1770s, it was not a revival of Puritanism or the afterglow of the Great Awakening that made it meaningful to remind Yankees of the "errand into the wilderness," to jar them with the jeremiad's convincing power, to call them to do battle with Antichrist, and to offer them the consolation of the millennium. Each of these styles remained "authentic" because they came to symbolize a new reality: that history was primarily civic, that the story of nations turned on the success of liberty, and that only a virtuous body politic could withstand the corruption of balanced government. In this light, religion does serve an important function in the 1770s, but not as a prophetic voice calling for a new political agenda. The images and myths of the traditional Puritan forms renewed their vitality by deferring to certain prevailing intellectual currents. In sum, the clergy came to sustain republican political values as religious priorities.[41]

This pattern will become evident by studying the cler-

40. In analyzing contemporary religion, the sociologist Peter Berger has provided extremely helpful categories by which to understand how the same religious language takes on entirely different meanings in a new social and intellectual context. The "secular" theologians of today, for example, have taken the traditional vocabulary of Christianity and translated it according to the grammars of existentialism, psychoanalysis, sociology, and linguistic analysis. See "A Sociological View of the Secularization of Theology," *Journal for the Scientific Study of Religion* 6 (1967): 3–16; and *A Rumor of Angels: Modern Society and the Rediscovery of the Supernatural* (New York, 1969).

41. While Jonathan Edwards and others of his generation had absorbed the ideas of Newton and Locke—with profound consequences for theology—this generation internalized "Country" ideology. But while Edwards had kept the new learning subservient to traditional values, the emphasis was reversed after the 1750s. An important factor in this change is the contrasting degree of intellectual self-consciousness. Edwards was quite aware of the specific contemporary forms integrated into his thought and could verbalize their overall impact. Revolutionary clergymen, on the other hand, were being swept along by prevailing currents of thought while they denied ever letting go of the moorings of traditional New England religion.

gy's reconstruction of their own past and their redefinition of their own sense of mission, present and future. It is ironic that a century earlier New England maintained its sense of collective superiority by withdrawing from the arena of English politics; but in the age of the American Revolution the region was able to sustain that sense of destiny only as it politicized even its religious values according to a British model.

ṽ

Few Americans attempted to resolve the political disputes of the 1770s by appeals to abstract political theory.[42] Their conceptual vocabulary found its deepest roots in history—biblical, classical, Renaissance, and most importantly English—and their self-understanding came primarily from the nature of this historical awareness. New Englanders in particular appealed to the precedents of history for wisdom to sort out contemporary issues. Their own self-conscious traditionalism both as Britons and New Englanders predisposed them to argue any point, religious or political, from the lessons of history. From their perspective the course of history was a continuous stream channeled at any given point by the same basic issues. Thus James Lovell, the well-known Boston schoolmaster and future Congressman, feared the dire consequences that ensued from a society's abolishing its militia because he knew from "historical facts" that "the same causes will, in similar circumstances, forever produce the same effects."[43] With similar logic Charles Turner, pastor at Duxbury, reassured an audience gathered to honor the Pilgrims that God would continue to manifest his favor to New England:

42. Bailyn, *The Ideological Origins of the American Revolution*, pp. 27–28; Pocock, "Civic Humanism and its Role in Anglo-American Thought," in *Politics, Language and Time* (New York, 1971), p. 96.

43. Lovell, *An Oration Delivered April 2d, 1771*, p. 8.

... when God has seen fit to appear for a people, for several ages, in a remarkable manner, there is a certain degree of probability, according to the known rules of analogy, that he will continue to remarkably favor them.[44]

This most basic assumption that what happened yesterday will come to pass again makes the study of historical perspectives crucial in coming to terms with the critical religious and political values of Revolutionary New England.

The scheme of history by which the patriots of New England captured the past was not cluttered with loose ends. Their perception of the course of events since the Reformation blended simplicity and comprehensiveness. In politics or religion, as a collectivity or as individuals, the advance of mankind was measured by one simple gauge: the comparative success or failure of liberty, with liberty defined as that capacity to enjoy one's own public and private life within limits set by defined law rather than by the arbitrary will of those in power.[45] This concept of history as a dynamic struggle between a spirit of freedom and the "arbitrary spirit of lawless ambition" was the key that unlocked the door of understanding to all of history, from the smallest personal endeavor to the rise and fall of empires. Since the time of the "dark ages" when liberty and virtue apparently had deserted the earth in favor of ignorance, superstition, and "ungovernable power," men throughout Europe, but especially in England, gradually grew more impatient in their bondage and determined at all cost to become "CHRIST'S *freemen.*"[46]

44. Turner, *A Sermon Preached at Plymouth*, p. 34; see also Bailyn, *The Ideological Origins of the American Revolution*, p. 85.

45. Ibid., p. 77; David L. Jacobson, ed., *The English Libertarian Heritage* (Indianapolis, Ind., 1965), p. xxxvi; Howard, *A Sermon Preached to the Ancient and Honorable Artillery-Company*, p. 9.

46. Johnson, *Some Important Observations*, p. 7; John Adams, *A Dissertation on the Canon and Feudal Law*, in *The Works of John Adams . . .*, ed.

This vision of history was able to emcompass everything from the Reformation to the Stamp Act because of
the dual nature of liberty. Following the age-old theory of
the two swords of authority, Yankees pictured the battle
between power and liberty on two interrelated but separate fronts, the civil and religious. The confederacy between these two systems of tyranny and their successive
engagements with the forces of civil and religious liberty
were articulated most explicitly by John Adams in
1765,[47] but recounted scores of times by ministers during
the war. It was the canon and feudal law—synonyms for
ecclesiastical and civil tyranny—which since the Reformation had carried on a two-pronged attack on English
liberty. The spiritual tyranny of the papacy aligned with
the civil despotism of Spain and France—as well as their
minions the Stuarts—explained every jot and tittle of the
experience of England, both Old and New.[48]

In reflecting on the previous two centuries, Revolutionary New England could account for the rise of liberty,
both civil and religious, in a number of remarkable ways:
the defeat of the Armada, the overthrow of the Stuarts,
the Glorious Revolution (with the ousting of that tyrant
and "biggoted papist" Sir Edmund Andros),[49] the
Hanoverian succession, the defeats of the Pretender in
Britain and the French in Canada. In each of these cases
the battle lines were clearly drawn between liberty and
Protestantism on the one side and the "two sister furies,"
popery and arbitary power, on the other.[50] Was it any
wonder that New England ministers saw the Stamp Act

Charles Francis Adams (Boston, 1851), 3:451; Elisha Fish, *Joy and Gladness: A Thanksgiving Discourse Preached in Upton, May 28, 1766* . . . (Providence, R. I., 1767), p. 17.
    47. John Adams, *A Dissertation*, pp. 448–64.
    48. Emerson, *A Thanksgiving Sermon*, pp. 19–29; Amos Adams, *Religious
Liberty*, pp. 12–40.
    49. Amos Adams, *A Concise, Historical View* . . . (Boston, 1774), p. 25.
    50. William Symmes, *A Sermon, Delivered at Andover* (Salem, Mass.,
1769), p. 11.

and the proposed Anglican bishopric as only different branches of the same scheme of tyranny[51] or that they genuinely feared that behind the later restrictive taxations there were designs "forming to dethrone his present majesty, king George the third . . . and to introduce the Pretender, and with him the popish religion . . . ?[52] The defense of civil and religious liberty against popery and slavery was the thread which united all of history and gave substance to extended comparisons between Revolutionary events and the heritage of freeborn Britons.[53]

When Samuel Adams suggested in 1772 that the "Religion and public liberty of a People are intimately connected . . . and therefore rise and fall together," he was reflecting the common assumption that liberty always had a religious as well as a civil dimension. Similarly, when he suggested that above everything else New England should fear the dangers of popery, he expressed the assumption that corruption, the foe of liberty, did battle within the church as well as the state.[54] It made sense for him, as it did for his clerical colleague in Boston radicalism, Samuel Cooper, that Roman Catholicism was "the extremest despotism," and functioned as the spiritual agent of the universal plot to enslave mankind.[55] This kind of intense antipapal rhetoric, which was commonplace in the Revolutionary period, makes sense only

51. Carl Bridenbaugh, *Mitre and Sceptre: Transatlantic Faiths, Ideas, Personalities, and Politics 1689–1775* (New York, 1962), p. 259; Arthur L. Cross, *The Anglican Episcopate and the American Colonies* (New York, 1902), pp. 139–60; Bailyn, *The Ideological Origins of the American Revolution*, p. 97.

52. Peter Whitney, *The Transgression of a Land Punished by a Multitude of Rulers* (Boston, 1774), pp. 61–62; Ebenezer Baldwin, *The Duty of Rejoicing under Calamities and Afflictions* . . . (New York, 1776), p. 27.

53. Emerson, *A Thanksgiving Sermon*, pp. 13–30.

54. Samuel Adams in *The Writings of Samuel Adams*, ed. H. A. Cushing, 2 (New York, 1906), 336; 1 (New York, 1904), 201–202.

55. Samuel Cooper, *A Discourse on the Man of Sin* (Boston, 1774), p. 66. See Charles W. Akers, "The Lost Reputation of Samuel Cooper as a Leader of the American Revolution," *The New England Historical and Genealogical Register* 130 (1976): 23–34.

as one comprehends the new terms into which it had been translated by the categories of opposition political thought. A traditional religious vocabulary became highly credible for many because, as Peter Thacher pointed out to the Massachusetts Provincial Council in 1776, "Miter'd hypocrites, and cringing, base-souled Priests, have impiously dared to enlist the oracles of God into the service of despotism"—in other words, Catholics were doing the bidding of tyrannical masters. It was no wonder that Peter Whitney, in the same sermon, could attribute the problems of the British administration both to new heights of legislative corruption and to secret designs for reestablishing popery.[56]

What is noteworthy about anti-Catholic sentiment in this context is its fear of Catholic weakness rather than strength. Whereas John Locke had argued that Catholics should be denied toleration because of their allegiance to the Pope rather than to the state,[57] Revolutionary ministers were afraid that Whitehall's power-hungry courtiers would exploit the church hierarchy for their own designs. New England's volcanic reaction to the Quebec Act of 1774, for instance, sprang from the assumption that despots would use a servile form of religion "to cut off all the liberties of the colonies." Samuel Langdon complained that Catholicism had been expanded in Canada "to serve political purposes."[58] Carrying this point a step farther, Ebenezer Baldwin surmised that New England religion retained far too much liberty for Britain's grasping rulers:

the British Ministry will therefore find it necessary in order to establish their System of civil Government, to introduce some different kind of

---

56. Whitney, *The Transgression of a Land*, pp. 61–62, 69.

57. John Miller, *Popery and Politics in England, 1660–1688* (Cambridge, 1973), p. 88.

58. John Lathrop, *A Discourse Preached December 15th, 1774* . . . (Boston, 1774), p. 28; Langdon, *Government Corrupted*, p. 28.

Religion: And the indulgent Favour shewn to Popery, by establishing it in Canada, may justly fill us with fearful Apprehensions of what their despotic Principles may lead them to.[59]

This rhetoric did not derive primarily from old Puritan fears that Rome pulled the strings for Stuart puppets or from Enlightenment attacks that priests hoped to keep mankind in the dark ages. Rather, it stemmed from a view of history that had come to define the struggle between Protestants and Catholics as one battle in the larger war between liberty and arbitrary power.

In this interpretive environment, one theme above all others seemed to recapture the energy of past heroic action. The myth of the "errand into the wilderness" long had woven a certain magic spell for New Englanders,[60] but the disintegration of Anglo-American relations evoked a wave of filiopietism about New England origins which became the most distinctive theme of Revolutionary sermons. Institutionalized in the Plymouth Anniversary Sermons from 1773 to 1780,[61] but explicit also in nearly every printed pulpit address, the question of why the forefathers came to America sounded as a constant reminder that patriots must imitate their noble ancestors. Ministers would not let their congregations forget the "howling wilderness," the "cruel savages," the "severest hardships," "the stubborn glebe."[62] Most importantly, they pointed to those noble motives of the forefathers which in the jeremiad tradition had always quickened the beat of New England hearts.

However parallel these evoked feelings of awe and

59. Baldwin, *The Duty of Rejoicing*, p. 27.
60. Wesley Frank Craven, *The Legend of the Founding Fathers* (New York, 1956), pp. 1–32.
61. Ibid., pp. 35–39.
62. Timothy Hilliard, *The Duty of a People under the Oppression of Man* ... (Boston, 1774), p. 23; Johnson, *Some Important Observations*, p. 56; Warren, *An Oration, Delivered March 5th, 1772*, pp. 16–17.

admiration were to those of the earlier tradition, the redefinition of the Puritans' motives was a far cry from the traditional eulogy of the jeremiad. Interpreting history always by explicit analogy, and thus identifying the motives of their ancestors with their own, New Englanders feared that "the same greedy insatiable monster, from which the gospel fled to this wilderness for shelter, as the dove to the thicket . . . the same monster, tyranny, is on his way to seize and devour."[63] Because the founders of New England had "nobly resolved never to wear the yoke of despotism," had abandoned an indolent European world "falling prey to tyranny," and had transmitted this heritage at great cost to their descendants, the contemporary generation could hardly submit to arbitrary and despotic power.[64] The pulpit's theme continued to be that "liberty was the noble errand of our fathers over the Atlantic," and men were left with the direct implication that God would "still continue to support and preserve it."[65] This clear imposition of civic humanism upon a century-old Puritan idiom was expressed in purest form by Joseph Warren, who argued that the first settlers came to America because of outrages committed on a balanced constitution in their native land;[66] and by Gad Hitchcock, who actually judged the religion of the first settlers by the extent to which they promoted civil liberty:

If religion is eminently productive of liberty, and the security of it; we are led, from the remarkable display of liberty in the great undertaking of our fore-fathers, to form a favorable judgment of their religion.[67]

---

63. Jonathan Bascom, *A Sermon Preached at Eastham* . . . (Boston, 1775), p. 19.
64. Joseph Warren, *An Oration, Delivered March 6, 1775* (Newport, R. I., 1775), p. 6; Hilliard, *The Duty of a People*, p. 23.
65. Amos Adams, *A Concise, Historical View*, p. 49.
66. Warren, *An Oration, Delivered March 5th, 1772*, p. 7.
67. Hitchcock, *A Sermon Preached at Plymouth*, p. 35.

Most sermons, however, pointed to similar ends by a less obvious translation of Puritan rhetoric. Ministers commonly assumed that it was not to be "concealed or denied, that our progenitors were persecuted mainly on account of their religious sentiments and practice."[68] Yet in elaborating on the meaning of this, ministers of the 1770s reflected once again the evolution towards libertarian perceptions of all social questions. The mainspring of the forefathers' religion became closely aligned, if not identified, with the privileges of religious liberty. The purest religious motive of the first American Puritans was their commitment to *free liberty of conscience to worship God in their own way*."[69] They had fled the "blasting frowns of tyranny," the "yoke of despotism," and the "rage of prelatical tyranny and persecution." They were harried from England's shores by that "grand enemy of civil and religious liberty," Archbishop Laud.[70] In sum, the Puritan faced the same dual threat to liberty confronted by the anxious American patriot. New Englanders of the 1770s were thus called to "adopt every self-denying measure, and call forth every magnanimous exertion" in direct imitation of their renowned forefathers, those "free-born spirits," whose voices still cried from the ground, "My Sons, scorn to be SLAVES!"[71]

In redefining the content of the errand in terms of the struggle between power and liberty, clergymen used the

68. Samuel Baldwin, *A Sermon Preached at Plymouth, December 22, 1775* (Boston, 1776), p. 24.

69. Adams, *Religious Liberty*, p. 25.

70. Warren, *An Oration, Delivered March 5th, 1772*, p. 16; Warren, *An Oration, Delivered March 6, 1775* (Newport, R. I., 1775), p. 6; West, *A Sermon Preached before the Honorable Council*, p. 57; Adams, *A Concise, Historical View*, p. 14.

71. Hitchcock, *A Sermon Preached at Plymouth*, p. 17; Warren, *An Oration, Delivered March 5th, 1772*, p. 17.

evocative potential of this myth for ends quite different from those of the traditional jeremiad. Rather than heightening the moral distinction between the contemporary generation and their noble progenitors, the new myth above all reconfirmed contemporary values. Instead of issuing a prophetic judgment of the present and an appeal to return to the solid virtues of the forefathers, Revolutionary ministers confidently projected their own sense of identity upon the past. The sense of history that found Puritans decked out in eighteenth-century garb seemed to offer providential sanction to the War for Independence. God has "always owned the cause of liberty in North America," boasted Judah Champion of Litchfield, Connecticut, "and will continue to own it." How could there be any doubt that he would vindicate America, the new embodiment of that cause for which God had sifted a whole nation and separated its finest grain?[72]

Although the Revolutionary clergy never failed to believe that their cause was eminently just and good, they did qualify that optimism with the lingering fear "that nothing can prevent our success, but only our sins."[73] They did invoke the jeremiad to mitigate the detrimental effects of irreligion and vice upon the body politic. This theme of apostasy, however, did not strike chords of response because the reigning beliefs of the Revolutionary generation were still original sin and the need of grace.[74] As prevalent as these doctrines were in certain circles, the real sense of crisis at the heart of the patriot

72. Champion, *A Brief View of the Distresses, Hardships and Dangers,* pp. 6, 28–29. Having redefined God's primary purpose in peopling America as the preservation of civil and religious liberty, New Englanders had good reason to think of God's New Israel as thirteen colonies rather than three or four.
73. West, *A Sermon Preached before the Honorable Council,* p. 57.
74. Miller, "From the Covenant to the Revival," p. 342.

cause sprang from the sudden encroachments of arbitrary power rather than from any intense conviction of sin. The primary temptation for New Englanders was to "silently give up our liberties" and thus "degenerate from the noble principles of our ancestors."[75] The clearest moral standards delineated by the pulpit related to the question of whether or not a man would "stand fast in the liberty wherewith Christ has made him free." According to Samuel Sherwood,

There is but one general distinction that is of essential importance in the cause now depending, and that is to be made by drawing the dividing line between the true friends to the rights of humanity,—our dear country, and constitutional liberties and privileges, civil and religious: And the base traiterous [sic] and perfidious enemies thereto.[76]

Within this framework, where morality became defined primarily in terms of liberty, ministers still found a sizable role for the traditional jeremiad with its focus on individual sin. Invectives against personal vice and shortcomings made sense, realizing "that for the sins of a people God may suffer the best government to be corrupted or entirely dissolved." The increase of vice "gradually tends to corrupt the constitution, and in time brings on it's [sic] dissolution."[77] According to Stephen Johnson, great iniquity rather than bribery and corruption was the only way that "a people free by nature, and by civil constitution" could be brought into bondage. In a

75. Patten, A Discourse Delivered at Hallifax, p. 16.
76. Sherwood, A Sermon, Containing Scriptural Instructions, p. ix. According to J. G. A. Pocock, "the jeremiad—the most American of all rhetorical modes—was merged with the language of the classical republican theory to the point where one can almost speak of an apocalyptic Machiavellism; and this too heightened the tendency to see that moment at which corruption threatened America as one of unique and universal crisis" (The Machiavellian Moment, p. 513).
77. Langdon, Government Corrupted, pp. 10–11, 12.

similar vein, Samuel West proposed that if "a spirit of repentance and reformation [could] prevail through the land, I should not have the least apprehension or fear of being brought under the iron rod of slavery."[78] Thus, the traditional rhetoric of the jeremiad was marshaled for new purposes both when it condemned those refusing to follow liberty and when vice—traditionally defined— was denounced as the first step toward political corruption. In sum, Yankees renewed the jeremiad because the dread of tyranny gripped them as much as the need for repentance ever had.

᳇

New England clergymen justified the fight for American independence as a last-ditch effort to preserve those values for which Britain's ancient constitution seemed to stand. By issuing a call to arms, they self-consciously continued the "noble struggles for liberty" which had ever been Britain's greatest glory, but which she had forfeited to vice, corruption, and arbitrary power. The Americans thereby were pursuing "the glorious cause in which Great-Britain herself, has frequently and strenuously contended against tyrants and oppressors."[79] In direct imitation of those principles which had long protected Britain's excellent constitution, Americans took up arms against a system governed by "opposite principles." Britain's "unnatural war waged against her own children to establish arbitrary power" confirmed beyond question that Britons were denying their own self-identity. In determining to preserve and maintain this threatened British heritage, Americans, far from delighting in the

78. West, A Sermon Preached before the Honorable Council, p. 57.
79. Keteltas, God Arising and Pleading, p. 20.

New World itself, hoped to salvage the liberty of the Old.[80]

The American conviction that Britain had rejected her birthright of liberty evolved surprisingly late. For the duration of the Anglo-French wars and well into the 1760s, New Englanders maintained an almost untarnished idealization of the British constitution. Britain remained the "favorite nation" of divine providence, possessing an equitable government envied by all free people. With the defeat of French tyranny freshly in mind, New Englanders had never been more warmly "attached to those privileges which are the Birth-right of *British* Subjects."[81] In applauding the accomplishments of Hanoverians, "the Scourge of Tyrants," and faithful guardians of civil and religious liberty, New Englanders interpreted history as a moral spectrum extending from tyranny and slavery on the one hand to political virtue and liberty on the other. In contrast to certain opposition publicists, the pulpit before 1765 remained firmly attached to the ideal that Britain was the epitome of freedom. The clergy's ears were still attentive to threats of French popery and slavery. In contrast to King George, "whose Hands were never stained with Bribery and Oppression," the French continued to be identified as the "implacable Enemy" to British liberty and religion. It was not until the Stamp Act crisis that New England

---

80. Ibid., pp. 21–22. Many scholars, including Alan Heimert, William G. McLoughlin, and Sacvan Bercovitch, have argued the contrary: that the Revolution was the final expression of a growing moral dichotomy between America and Britain that had been building since the Great Awakening. For a representative statement of this view, see McLoughlin, "The Role of Religion in the Revolution," in *Essays on the American Revolution,* ed. Stephen G. Kurtz and James H. Hutson, (Chapel Hill, N.C., 1973), pp. 197–203.

81. Samuel Langdon, *Joy and Gratitude to God* . . . (Portsmouth, N. H., 1760), p. 23; Benjamin Stevens, *A Sermon Preached at Boston* . . . (Boston, 1761), p. 56; Samuel Cooper, *A Sermon Preached before His Excellency Thomas Pownall* . . . (Boston, 1759), p. 23.

became convinced that the ever-present plots and schemes of tyranny were as much a domestic as a foreign problem for the British nation.[82]

Despite the tendency of radical Whigs to suspect clandestine schemes and hidden motives, it was painful for New England to give up its image of Britain as the foremost bastion of freedom. Without question ministers perceived the Stamp Act as part of an insidious design to enslave the colonies,[83] but remarkably they refrained from attributing the scheme to a fundamental breakdown of the balanced constitution. Even after 1765 the mixed government of Britain still appeared to function as the most perfect form of rule imaginable in an imperfect world. The clergy still had "too great affection for our gracious King" and "too high veneration for the Parliament and . . . their friendly disposition towards America" to entertain the idea that the Stamp Act originated from either of them:

We rather believe that it obtained a *parliamentary* faction, thro' the deceitful plausibility, and the specious glossing lies, of some individu-

---

82. Samuel Haven, *The Supreme Influence of the Son of God . . .* (Portsmouth, N. H., 1761), p. 20; Mather Byles, *A Sermon Delivered March 6th 1760 . . .* (New London, Conn., 1760), p. 15; Cooper, *A Sermon Preached before His Excellency Thomas Pownall,* p. 47.

83. The members of the clergy appear to have attributed the Stamp Act to a London plot more readily than do secular publicists, who at this time were more likely to locate the truly corrupt conspirators in the colonial stamp masters rather than in the British court. This may well imply that traditional Puritan categories predisposed ministers to interpret specific political grievances as part of the larger moral struggle between good and evil, liberty and power, a conviction not reached by many American patriots until a succession of British encroachments convinced them that an all-encompassing and premeditated scheme existed. For clergymen who attributed the Stamp Act to a comprehensive plot hatched across the Atlantic, see Emerson, *A Thanksgiving Sermon;* and Johnson, *Some Important Observations.* The thrust of secular pamphlets is available in Edmund S. Morgan, ed., *Prologue to Revolution: Sources and Documents on the Stamp Act Crisis, 1764–1766* (Chapel Hill, N. C., 1959); and Bernard Bailyn, ed., *Pamphlets of the American Revolution, 1750–1776* (Cambridge, Mass., 1965).

als, the first contrivers of it, who were enemies to the nation, and,
for ought I know, had an hidden intent of plunging *Great Britain* and
her colonies into one common destruction.[84]

Other clergymen agreed with these opinions of Henry
Cumings that indeed only a faction, a "Frenchified party
in the nation," could have manipulated this legislation,
which if fully understood would have been abhorrent to
the king, Parliament and people of Great Britain.[85] New
Englanders feared that behind these misguided counsels
lay the cunning of French tyranny, still unable to relin-
quish its hopes of enslaving the British Isles. For several
ministers the most awesome fear aroused by the Stamp
Act was not that Britain and the colonies would go to
war, but that such a conflict would lead to the French
domination of Great Britain.[86] As long as arbitrary
power remained a foreign menace, New Englanders continued to identify themselves with the "happy and excellent constitution" of "British Israel."[87] In the wake of the
Stamp Act, however, the intense bonds of loyalty to
Britain began to crumble. That there had been "gradual
encroachments" of corruption and bribery upon British
government led to more awesome speculations that a
"venal spirit of corruption" might someday reign in the
British court.[88]

It is unnecessary, or hardly possible, to correlate precisely the erosion of New England's confidence in British
liberty with the succeeding storms of political debate
which characterized the decade prior to the "shot heard

84. Cumings, *A Thanksgiving Sermon,* pp. 19–20.

85. Johnson, *Some Important Observations,* p. 15.

86. Emerson, *A Thanksgiving Sermon,* p. 14; Patten, *A Discourse Delivered at Hallifax,* p. 21; Cumings, *A Thanksgiving Sermon,* pp. 19–20.

87. Eliphalet Williams, *A Sermon Preached in the Audience of the General
Assembly* . . . (Hartford, 1763), p. 27; Nathaniel Appleton, *A Thanksgiving
Sermon on the Total Repeal of the Stamp-Act* (Boston, 1766), p. 23.

88. Johnson, *Some Important Observations,* p. 11.

round the world." With each new crisis, the clamor of fear and despair grew more intense until by the outbreak of fighting the once mellow tones of pride and confidence in British institutions could no longer be heard. For the clergy, at least, the darker side of opposition ideology—the firm conviction that Britain was deluded with a "mere phantom of liberty," "a mere shadow of it's [sic] ancient political system"—surfaced only when a series of restrictive measures by the British government convinced them that a spirit of tyranny did in fact determine public policy.[89] Most importantly, the primary threat of corruption remained external to the American colonies themselves, giving substance to a growing moral distinction between the Old World and the New. As liberty seemed to take its leave from Britain, America as never before became the asylum of liberty and the seat of Christ's advancing kingdom.[90]

For New England clergymen the real intellectual revolution triggered by the break with England was the identification of cosmic evil with that which at the end of the Great War for the Empire had been the symbol of right and virtue—the British system of government.[91] "We have lived to see the time . . . when that constitution of government which has so long been the glory and strength of the English nation, is deeply undermined and ready to tumble into ruins," lamented Samuel Langdon in

89. Langdon, *Government Corrupted*, p. 16.
90. Jack P. Greene, "Political Mimesis: A Consideration of the Historical and Cultural Roots of Legislative Behavior in the British Colonies in the Eighteenth Century," *American Historical Review* 75 (1969): 359–60.
91. I would see the fundamental transfer in priorities from religion to politics as an earlier development than does Edmund S. Morgan. By 1760 New England ministers had already expanded the implications of political understanding into all forms of discourse. The major intellectual revolution for them after 1765 was the identification of Britain as a primary symbol of moral evil. See "The American Revolution Considered as an Intellectual Movement," in *Paths of American Thought*, ed. Arthur M. Schlesinger, Jr., and Morton White (Boston, 1963), pp. 11–33.

the Massachusetts Election Sermon of 1775.[92] On the same occasion the following year, Samuel West saw nothing but the fallen ruins. The "wanton execution of arbitrary power" and the "barbarity unknown to Turks and Mahometan infidels" led him to conclude that the tyranny which issued from London was nothing other than the rage and fury of the "horrible wild beast" of John's Revelation.[93] The assumption of Britain's total depravity made sense to clergymen who had witnessed in a single decade such indisputable signs of tyranny as a tax to promote ignorance, a vast array of new placemen and pensioners, a design to support popery in North America, the elimination of trial by one's peers, the imposition of rule by a standing army, and finally plunder and massacre by mercenary soldiers. The pulpit could no longer deny that the nation which once offered a firm refuge for the oppressed now stood as a stronghold of arbitrary power.

This intellectual revolution, which transformed "British Israel" into "Assyria" and the servants of God into the offspring of "their father the Devil," expanded and intensified cosmic interpretations of the Revolution.[94] The assumption that liberty had abandoned Britain created both a new rhetoric of Antichrist and a new awareness of the coming millennium.

In two sermons during 1776, both of which despaired of liberty maintaining any influence in British government, the rationalist Samuel West and the New Light Samuel Sherwood broke with their Protestant heritage and advanced the most innovative theology of the future since the Reformation. By slightly different logic both

92. Langdon, *Government Corrupted*, p. 6.
93. West, *A Sermon Preached before the Honorable Council*, pp. 53, 63.
94. Nicholas Street, *The American States Acting Over the Part of the Children of Israel in the Wilderness* . . . (New Haven, Conn., 1777), p. 34; Elijah Fitch, *A Discourse, the Substance of Which was Delivered at Hopkinton* . . . (Boston, 1776), pp. 6–7.

men reached the conclusion that the "horrible wild beast" of Revelation 13 applied to British tyranny rather than to the Pope and the Church of Rome. According to Samuel Sherwood, these prophecies could not be confined "to so narrow a circle, as papal Rome," but applied to "another persecuting tyrannical power," namely "the corrupt system of tyranny and oppression, that has been fabricated and adopted by the ministry and parliament of Great Britain."[95] Similarly, West understood that "the description of every part of this beast will answer better to be understood of political, than ecclesiastical tyrants."[96] By thus translating the rhetoric of Antichrist into terms comprehensible to stalwart defenders of liberty, both ministers appealed to the deepest spiritual sensitivities of their audience and demanded tangible proof of indignation against this tool of Satan. With Britain's flagrant corruption in full view, Samuel West denounced her as Satan's ambassador:

Does it not then highly concern us all to stand fast in the liberty wherewith Heaven hath made us free, and to strive to get the victory over the beast and his image, over every species of tyranny?[97]

A surprising vein of millennial expectancy also surfaced early in the conflict. But in contrast to the French wars, when millennial hope seemed to follow military success, these expectations of a new age appeared when the war effort was still in its darkest hour. Ebenezer Baldwin, who contracted a fatal disease during the British invasion of New York, had predicted as early as November 1775 that the American colonies would be the

95. Sherwood, *The Church's Flight into the Wilderness*, pp. 14–15.
96. West, *A Sermon Preached before the Honorable Council*, p. 63.
97. Ibid., p. 67.

"Foundation of a great and mighty Empire . . . which shall be the principal Seat of that glorious Kingdom, which Christ shall erect upon Earth in the latter Days."[98] The basis of his hope once again reveals the pattern that political concerns were instrumental in renewing sacred rhetoric. Baldwin believed that the War for Independence was bringing on the final days because in America "the Principles of Liberty [were] to be better examined, than in the Foundation of any other Empire." Taking for granted that liberty had abandoned Europe and now traveled westward, Baldwin reasoned that the ferment of the war itself would "prove the Means of fixing and establishing Liberty upon the most permanent Basis."[99] America was freedom's last asylum and thus, despite gloomy military prospects, the center of God's redemptive plan. With the same assumption that liberty was "expiring and gasping for life" in Britain, other ministers concluded that America would become her permanent sanctuary since God would not allow liberty to be banished from the earth.[100] And because the future of liberty, the cause of God, depended entirely upon the war's outcome, the conflict assumed all the emotional intensity of a crusade of heaven against hell. Americans were not fighting for themselves, but for the well-being of the whole world and "millions upon millions of our posterity . . . Let us then arouse to arms!" thundered Peter Thacher, who not only served as chaplain of the Massachusetts Provincial Council in 1775 but had also raised a company of soldiers in Malden,

98. Baldwin, *The Duty of Rejoicing,* p. 38. A Yale graduate of 1763, Baldwin served the First Congregational Church of Danbury, Connecticut. He joined the militia of that town for the defense of New York in the summer of 1776.
99. Ibid., pp. 39, 40.
100. West, *A Sermon Preached before the Honorable Council,* p. 58.

For, upon our exertions, under God, depends their freedom, upon our exertions depends the important question, whether the rising empire of America, shall be an empire of slaves or of freemen.[101]

Throughout the war, descriptions of America as the refuge of liberty galvanized New England's attention to millennial themes. Whereas the possibility of British victory evoked the dread that liberty—that "heaven-born virgin"—would be "rejected and despised of men," banished from an ungrateful world like the firstborn of God, the prospect of American success raised hopes that she would become "an asylum for the oppressed and persecuted of every country," and an example to "rouse a Spirit of liberty through other nations." The universal adoption of those principles for which the Americans fought would thus "turn a vale of tears, into a paradise of God."[102]

As Americans began to achieve military success against the British, the realization of such hopes seemed almost within reach. After the victory at Saratoga, Phillips Payson of Chelsea found the future glory of America "ravishing and transporting to the mind." Having emerged from the "deluges of the old world, drowned in luxury and lewd excess," America enjoyed "the purest liberty," a delight to God, a refuge to the oppressed and the envy of tyrants and the devil.[103] The following year the Universalist John Murray gave thanks for the same decisive victory because God had not allowed the cause of freedom to be crushed in embryo. He had preserved the struggling forces on whose success liberty depended, and thus it seemed far more plausible than before that

101. Thacher, *An Oration Delivered at Watertown*, p. 14.
102. Howard, *A Sermon Preached before the Honorable Council*, pp. 41–42; Keteltas, *God Arising and Pleading*, p. 20.
103. Payson, *A Sermon Preached before the Honorable Council*, p. 33.

America would become "IMMANUEL'S land—the seat of his kingdom till the sun shall fade."[104] In identifying the purposes of God with the struggle of liberty against unjust power, New England ministers had lowered the standard of millennial hope to a level attainable by American military victory.

The impact of such a victory upon the clergy's thinking again points out that political values were responsible for a compelling millennial vision. In a typical sermon celebrating complete American victory, Ezra Stiles identified America as God's new Israel primarily because her principles of government and religion had "realized the capital ideas of Harrington's Oceana."[105] In the infant republic Stiles took note of a spirit of "vigilance against corruption in purchasing elections," the continuation of "the wisdom of our ancestors in instituting a militia," "a free tenure of lands, an equitable distribution of property," effective means for "preserving and diffusing Knowledge among a people," and a firm commitment to "toleration and religious liberty."[106] This "triumph of LIBERTY on earth" led Stiles to conclude that the American Republic would illuminate the world with liberty. As other nations, in turn, looked to America as a model of government and religion, Stiles expected that the "progress of society will be accelerated by centuries . . . Light spreads from the day-spring in the west; and may it shine more and more until the perfect day."[107]

104. Murray, *Nehemiah, or the Struggle for Liberty*, p. 56.
105. Stiles, *The United States Elevated to Glory and Honor*, p. 8.
106. Ibid., pp. 33, 32, 8, 34, 52–53.
107. Ibid., pp. 98, 55, 52–53; see also Benjamin Trumbull, *God is to be Praised for the Glory of His Majesty* (New Haven, Conn., 1784). It took no great theological acumen for persons to be impressed with what seemed a clear relation between the Revolution and the millennium. Mrs. Hannah Winthrop, wife of the Harvard astronomer, wrote to Mercy Warren on January 9, 1778: "The grand Revolution of America may probably be big with consequences that will greatly effect [sic] the other hemisphere & make way for the

This exuberant confidence that America was the divine agent to initiate the millennium followed from the twofold assumption that history turned on the success of liberty and that the preservation of liberty turned on the outcome of the Revolution. What Alexis de Tocqueville said of a later generation of Americans had already taken shape in the minds of Stiles and his contemporaries: "The Americans combine the notions of Christianity and of liberty so intimately in their minds that it is impossible to make them conceive the one without the other."[108]

༄

No pattern of ideas brings into clearer focus the assimilation of Puritan categories by the tradition of radical Whiggery than those which Edmund Morgan has called the "Puritan ethic."[109] The long-established Puritan theme of eschewing wealth and luxury for the virtues of diligence and frugality gained new momentum when redirected as "an essential condition of political liberty."[110] For the New England clergy, as for John and Samuel Adams, the quest for personal accumulation was the antithesis of a spirit of liberty—the social prerequisite of any free government. Liberty "has the most to fear from . . . avarice; for it is no uncommon thing for a people to lose sight of their liberty in the eager pursuit of

---

accomplishment of those glorious Prophecies you mention. Some of these Prophecies lead us to expect a time when there shall be peace & love among all Mankind; but this can hardly be expected till the Gospel shall prevail universally." Mercy Otis Warren Papers, Massachusetts Historical Society. Henry May discusses this and similar connections between rationalism and the millennium in his chapter "Secular Millennialism" in *The Enlightenment in America* (New York, 1976), pp. 153–76.

108. Alexis de Tocqueville, *Democracy in America*, trans. Henry Reeve (New York, 1959), 1:317.

109. Edmund S. Morgan, "The Puritan Ethic and the American Revolution," *William and Mary Quarterly*, 3d Ser., 24 (1967): 3–43.

110. Ibid., pp. 9–10.

wealth."[111] Samuel Adams imagined that such dangers were being realized when he viewed "Conspirators against our Liberties" introducing "Levity Luxury & Indolence" into the colonies. This Puritan ethic held sway in the Revolutionary era not because Puritanism remained so dynamic, but because the Commonwealth tradition of politics was able to appropriate its vocabulary for political ends. Thus, while language remained essentially Puritan—"the love of money is the root of all evil"—the meanings attributed to it had been translated into what was essentially a "country ethic"—"covetousness is a fruitful source of corruption."[112]

The most intriguing facet of this intellectual shift is the amazing correspondence between Puritanism and the distinct form of republicanism which was nourished in the eighteenth-century Anglo-American world. Although various scholars have implied that this republicanism was a "more relaxed, secularized version" of Puritanism,[113] little effort has been given to explaining how one made way for the other. The fact that traditional New England vocabularies incorporated republican terms without substantive damage to Puritan forms does imply that the transition took place with a minimum of intellectual effort. New England's strong dissenting tradition, it seems, was particularly susceptible to the eighteenth-

111. Payson, *A Sermon Preached before the Honorable Council,* p. 12.

112. Adams, *The Writings of Samuel Adams,* 2: 267; Howard, *A Sermon Preached before the Honorable Council,* p. 30. This is not to say that New Englanders, under the tutelage of English radicals, understood political corruption only as executive manipulation of the legislature. Richard Bushman emphasizes that Massachusetts ideas of corruption never really outgrew their "origins in provincial politics with provincial emphasis on corruption as sheer greed." See Bushman, "Corruption and Power in Provincial America," in *The Development of a Revolutionary Mentality* (Washington, D. C., 1972), pp. 63–91; quotation on p. 83.

113. Wood, *The Creation of the American Republic,* p. 418; Edmund S. Morgan, ed., *Puritan Political Ideas* (Indianapolis, Ind., 1965), pp., xxxv–xlvii.

century Commonwealth tradition; common assumptions about human nature, society, and history allowed assimilation to occur almost unnoticed.

Yankees were able to draw the same lessons from history about human nature, whether they preferred the terms of sin and righteousness or corruption and virtue. When Samuel Adams declared "that ambition and lust of power above the law are . . . predominant passions in the breasts of most men,"[114] he expressed a view of human nature common to his Puritan forebears and the English libertarian heritage. His suspicion of human nature found deep roots both in the seventeenth-century Puritan assumption that "if each man may do what is good in his own eyes . . . there must of necessity follow the distraction and desolation of the whole," and in the opposition heritage, which, like *Cato's Letters,* suggested that men are controlled by their passions, "which being boundless and insatiable, are always terrible when they are not controlled."[115] Similarly, when clergymen issued a jeremiad with this theme of depravity in mind, they related collective virtue to the welfare of the state in a manner which found precedent in the Puritan covenant and the republican assumption that only a spirit of freedom could maintain a balanced constitution.

New England ministers also grounded their assumptions about the nature of society in these kindred traditions. In making the assertion that "parties and factions arising from false ambition, avarice or revenge . . . endanger the state," Phillips Payson could easily give the negative example of "the latter periods of the republic of Rome," or he could allude in a positive manner to the

114. Ibid., p. 60.
115. Stephen Foster, *Their Solitary Way: The Puritan Social Ethic in the First Century of Settlement in New England* (New Haven, Conn., 1971), p. 15; Jacobson, ed., *The English Libertarian Heritage,* p. 84.

exemplary harmony of New England's early settlers.[116] Likewise, when John Adams opposed the Stamp Act because it was "formed to strip us in great measure of the means of knowledge," he buttressed his defense of education both with the argument that "liberty cannot be preserved without general knowledge among the people," and with the example of his forefathers' wisdom in supporting schools and seminaries.[117] Even when New Englanders expressed their most common assumption about their own society, the conviction of collective superiority, they once again found ample evidence in the "errand into the wilderness" theme as well as the libertarian tradition that Britain's balanced constitution was the envy of the world. Similar assumptions about the nature of society allowed the descendants of the Puritans to argue for republican values without self-consciously altering their own sense of identity.

The most striking resemblance between traditional New England thought and the British pattern of opposition ideology is their understanding of the direction and significance of history. The historical vision of both was premised on the dynamic struggle between cosmic moral forces and the cyclical pattern of any society within that historical continuum. The apocalyptic battle against Antichrist was similar to the struggle of freeborn men against tyranny in that both presumed to be comprehensive explanations of history in which the participant could take a clear moral stand against evil. The darker side of both mentalities was expressed in exaggerated fears that devious schemes of evil were subverting the cause of truth in the world. In view of this moral struggle, men in either tradition were forced to constantly evaluate

---

116. Payson, *A Sermon Preached before the Honorable Council,* p. 22.
117. John Adams, *A Dissertation,* pp. 455–56.

whether their own society had degenerated from its pro-
fessed high principles. Both the jeremiad of the Puritan
covenant and the cyclical pattern of liberty outlined by
civic humanism feared that moral declension eventually
would be the demise of any virtuous people. The organic
concept of the state, in which each polity had an infancy,
manhood, and decline, made sense in a providential or a
cyclical model of history.[118] In view of these numerous
parallels, it is possible to suggest that one reason republicanism had such compelling appeal for New Englanders
is that they could follow its dictates without consciously
rejecting their past. The real similarities between John
Winthrop and James Burgh, for instance, or between
Cotton Mather and Thomas Hollis, allowed Yankees to
read the latter while still claiming the mantle of the
former. Furthermore, if opposition to Walpolean government was, as J. H. Plumb has said, "the one idealistic
feature of early eighteenth-century politics, the only political programme which could appeal to men with a sense
of moral purpose," then New England offered a most
hospitable intellectual environment.[119] If this opposition
tradition was, in fact, a modified seventeenth-century
vocabulary bred in the English Civil War,[120] it is little
wonder that eighteenth-century New England, whose
isolation and self-conscious traditionalism had for a century allowed the world to pass it by, found another
traditional vocabulary easy to assimilate. By different
routes two traditions out of step with the Walpolean

---

118. John G. Buchanan, "Puritan Philosophy of History From Restoration
to Revolution," *Essex Institute Historical Collections,* 104 (1968): 338;
Wood, *The Creation of the American Republic,* p. 29.

119. J. H. Plumb, *England in the Eighteenth Century* (Baltimore, Md.,
1950), p. 105.

120. Caroline Robbins, *The Eighteenth Century Commonwealthman*
(Cambridge, Mass., 1959), pp. 22–31; J. G. A. Pocock, *The Machiavellian
Moment,* pp. 361–400.

world converged in mid-eighteenth century America, their common heritage assuring a continued affinity.

This conflation, however, tells us even more about the course of republican thought in New England than about its origins. Other Americans without Puritan ancestors or sympathies became equally taken by a republican outlook. Recent studies indicate, in fact, that the purest strain of "Country" ideology is found in the philosophy of Jefferson and Madison, particularly as they came to oppose Hamilton's financial program in the 1790s.[121] They appropriated intact the arguments of English radical publicists and turned them against another ambitious executive and his mechanisms of corruption: standing armies, placemen and pensioners, chartered corporations, and an enormous public debt. Their vision of an agrarian republic certainly lays the strongest claim to being the true American heir of *Cato's Letters, The Craftsman,* and *The Independent Whig.* Political elites in New England, by contrast, developed a "dialect" of republican thought that never discarded a stern moral sense of civic functions. Having become republican without shedding certain reactionary religious assumptions, Yankees included many of these in their expectations for the United States. Whatever lessons other Americans drew from Sidney, Locke, and Harrington, Montesquieu, Bolingbroke, and Trenchard, New England clergymen during the War for Independence came away from these masters convinced that only a Christian republic could weather the storms of time. Was not Israel, rather than Rome, the ancient world's model republic?

---

121. See Lance Banning, "Republican Ideology and the Triumph of the Constitution, 1789 to 1793," *William and Mary Quarterly,* 31 (1974): 167–88; and Drew R. McCoy, "Republicanism and American Foreign Policy: James Madison and the Political Economy of Commercial Discrimination, 1789 to 1794," *William and Mary Quarterly* 31 (1974): 633–45.

Chapter Three

The Demand for a Republic of Christian Virtue: The Critical Period and the Moral Roots of New England Federalism

Statesmen may plan and speculate for liberty, but it is religion and morality alone which can establish the principles upon which freedom can securely stand.

Zabdiel Adams, 1782

Few New England clergymen throughout the eighteenth century avoided the charge that they made politics, rather than divinity, their study. Fewer still answered this accusation by retreating from the political implications of religion. "The religion, which we teach and promote," affirmed David Tappan, "is emphatically the guardian angel" of those privileges guaranteed by the commonwealth.[1] This pressing responsibility of civic oversight did not, however, impose a single pattern on the age which saw American and French citizens draw their swords against constituted authority. The political impact of religion in this era, in fact, provides a striking study in contrasts, a pattern of extremes unknown since Puritans of the previous century, on opposite shores of the Atlantic, simultaneously beheaded their king and founded a hierarchical community grounded in the assumptions of authority and deference. Reverend John Lathrop, for instance, the popular minister of Boston's Second Church, was wildly emotional about the cause of 1775 and, according to Governor Thomas Hutchinson, the most effective of the clergy in inflaming the people. By the 1790s, however, the Federalists chose him as chaplain of

1. David Tappan, *A Sermon, Delivered before the Annual Convention* . . . (Boston, 1797), p. 25.

97

the Massachusetts legislature and he inveighed with fury against France and Jefferson.[2]

Clergymen living during the last quarter of the eighteenth century could admire the accomplishments of both their revolutionary and authoritarian Puritan ancestors for several reasons. From the Scriptures they were fully aware of the moral extremes which human government could embody, from the God-ordained "higher powers" that executed divine judgment (Romans 13), to the demonic beast that would incur the same (Revelation 13). Moreover, such teaching was not mere theology for this generation of ministers. Within two decades, opinions shifted from one side of this spectrum to the other. In the 1770s the clergy associated the king with Antichrist and incited revolution with warnings that "Cursed be he that keepeth back his sword from blood." Their opponents identified these pulpits as "Gutters of Sedition," which channeled torrents of inflammatory abuse at constituted authority.[3] Never denying the charge, the clergy determined to dismantle British control with an invective that stretched both their Puritan and republican vocabularies.

That the American Revolution did strike the Antichrist of tyranny a decisive blow unfortunately did not eliminate the clergy's political anxieties. Steeped in republican history, they knew "that those persons and measures, which are important and beneficial in pulling down a despotic government, are often very incompetent and unfit to erect, support, or administer a government of freedom."[4] Such doubts about the viability of the new

2. See Clifford K. Shipton, *Sibley's Harvard Graduates,* 15 (Boston, 1970): 428–36.
3. Alice M. Baldwin, *The New England Clergy and the American Revolution* (Durham, N. C., 1928), pp. 127, 122.
4. David Tappan, *Christian Thankfulness* . . . (Boston, 1795), p. 28.

republic turned the clergy immediately to biblical themes of order, subordination, and honor. By the 1790s this search for stability in an increasingly uncertain world peaked in a veritable tidal wave of reaction. The sentiment that *"Order is Heaven's first law"* expressed the growing conviction of men whose religious images of civil authority came to picture rulers as "Ministers of God" deserving "titles of dignity, of awfulness, of sanctity, of divinity."[5] Men who could easily remember being compared to roundheads and levelers now used their religious authority to support openly those powers that were ordained by God—the Federalists—and in doing so reaped the charge of being "Priests made Politicians by Boston Tories."[6]

New England's reactions to both their own and the French Revolution have not gone wanting for able explanation. And clergymen in both eras have drawn more than their share of serious students, making the political ramifications of religion a tale told often and well.[7] But while great attention has focused on one age or the other, the relationship between them has remained a story largely undisclosed. Few historians, it seems, have asked

5. Joseph Lyman, *A Sermon, Preached before His Excellency James Bowdoin . . .* (Boston, 1787), p. 8; Timothy Dwight, *Virtuous Rulers a National Blessing . . .* (Hartford, 1791), pp. 32–34.

6. Anson Ely Morse, *The Federalist Party in Massachusetts to the Year 1800* (Princeton, N. J., 1909), p. 165.

7. The most important studies relating New England religion and the American Revolution are Baldwin, *The New England Clergy and the American Revolution;* Alan Heimert, *Religion and the American Mind: From the Great Awakening to the Revolution* (Cambridge, Mass., 1966); and Bernard Bailyn, "Religion and Revolution: Three Biographical Studies," in *Perspectives in American History* 4 (1970): 85–169. The religious dimensions of New England Federalism are explored in two dated but useful works, Morse, *The Federalist Party in Massachusetts to the Year 1800;* and Vernon Stauffer, *New England and the Bavarian Illuminati* (New York, 1918). The best single study of this subject is James M. Banner, Jr., *To the Hartford Convention: The Federalists and the Origins of Party Politics in Massachusetts, 1789–1815* (New York, 1970), especially chapters I and IV.

the question of how ministers who once breathed the fire of liberty became transformed into fearful traditionalists committed above all to the proposition that "innovations in government are dangerous."[8]

No one has seriously posed this question, basically an inquiry into the intellectual roots of clerical Federalism, precisely because no one has thought it deserved a serious answer. The jarring social, intellectual, and political dislocations of the 1790s have served as an airtight explanation of New England's desperate clutching after order and security. What more could be added to the turn-of-the-century conclusion of Anson Ely Morse that these external pressures were "the decisive factors" which led clergymen "to throw their weight into the scale of Federalism"?[9] Historians content with this completed puzzle have seen no reason to rearrange pieces and thus have delivered an explanation of clerical attachment to Federalism which stands in marked contrast to interpretations of those forces which two decades earlier molded the "black-coated regiment." Supposedly, ministers became revolutionaries due to a well-developed intellectual tradition that gave them little option but to thunder against tyranny, but they became Federalist due to a knee-jerk reaction to an uncertain world. Their cast of mind prior to 1789 has remained an answer without a question.[10]

This one-dimensional approach has implications reaching far beyond the political disposition of the clergy.

---

8. Zabdiel Adams, *A Sermon Preached before His Excellency John Hancock* . . . (Boston, 1782), p. 9.

9. Morse, *The Federalist Party in Massachusetts to the Year 1800*, p. 1.

10. In explaining the reaction of Yankee clergymen to the French Revolution, for example, neither Gary B. Nash nor J. Earl Thompson, Jr., has seen any reason to ask what forms were taking shape in New England thinking prior to the 1790s. See Nash, "The American Clergy and the French Revolution," *William and Mary Quarterly*, 3d Ser., 22 (1965): 392–412; and Thompson, "A Perilous Experiment: New England Clergymen and American Destiny, 1796–1826" (Ph.D. diss., Princeton University, 1966).

Recent studies of Federalist politics, even those which have concurred that New England Federalism "was a way of thought before it was a way of politics,"[11] have failed to probe deeply that pattern of understanding according to which Yankees perceived the tumultuous decade of the 1790s. Few iconoclasts have attempted to destroy the cherished image that 1789 is the student's proper chronological point of departure. Fortunately, advocates of the emerging republican synthesis have at least recognized the need to overcome that barrier,[12] but they have not gone on to explain adequately why the common path of republicanism divided at some point, leading some Americans toward Federalism and others in the direction of Jefferson. James M. Banner, Jr., for instance, has isolated four republican canons at the heart of Massachusetts Federalism: "virtue, harmony, carefully limited power, and an avoidance of foreign wars and entanglements," but has not explained what was distinctly Federalist about such goals which were equally cherished by Jeffersonians.[13] Richard Buel, Jr., has explained that distinction by suggesting that New England political elites were less secure in their relationship to the electorate than elsewhere in America. They clung to Federalist ideology to bolster their own raging doubts and to tone down a volatile electorate.[14] This explanation does carry considerable weight when applied to Yankee clergymen, who by the end of the Revolution were under considerable attack. The influential Peter Thacher, for instance, soon to be called to the prestigious Brattle Street

---

11. Banner, *To the Hartford Convention,* p. 3.

12. The importance of the republican tradition to the historian's understanding of politics in the 1790s is well documented by John R. Howe, Jr., "Republican Thought and the Political Violence of the 1790's," *American Quarterly* 19 (1967): 147–65; and Gordon S. Wood, *The Creation of the American Republic, 1776–1787* (Chapel Hill, N. C., 1969).

13. Banner, *To the Hartford Convention,* pp. 26–30.

14. Richard Buel, Jr., *Securing the Revolution: Ideology in American Politics, 1789–1815* (Ithaca, N. Y., 1972), pp. 81–85.

Church, came out openly in 1783 to challenge New England's disregard of her ministers:

The late contest with Great Britain, glorious as it hath been for their country, hath been peculiarly unfortunate for the clergy. Perhaps no set of men, whose hearts were so roughly engaged in it, or who contributed in so great a degree to its success, have suffered more by it. The people, having emancipated themselves from the British government, and felt their competence to carry every point they chose, have, in some places at least, forgotten that they could never be emancipated from the bonds of justice.[15]

The clergy clearly had the jitters, a classic case of status anxiety. Yet beyond this necessary factor in explaining the rise of Federalist ideology, we still need to understand what intellectual frameworks were available to these anxious men. What kind of values and attitudes could they appropriate to offer to themselves and their constituents a satisfying interpretation of the new republic's unsettled condition? To answer these questions, it is necessary to explore another dimension of New England Federalism, that characteristic dialect of republican conviction that came to the fore during the "Critical Period."[16]

ï

It was a long-awaited day when Timothy Dwight stood in the pulpit to reflect on the defeat of Cornwallis by the American army. Focusing on a prophetic text from Isaiah

15. Peter Thacher, *Observations upon the Present State of the Clergy in New-England* (Boston, 1783), p. 5.

16. For purposes of this chapter, the "Critical Period" refers generally to the time between the American and French Revolutions. Popularized by John Fiske a century ago in *The Critical Period of American History, 1783–1789* (Boston, 1888), this phrase was coined by John Quincy Adams in a commencement address at Harvard in 1787 and is a particularly appropriate description of New England apprehensions about the republican experiment in the 1780s. See Wood, *The Creation of the American Republic,* pp. 393–403. For an overview of historical interpretations of this period, see Richard B. Morris, "The Confederation Period and the American Historian," *William and Mary Quarterly,* 3d Ser., 13 (1956): 139–56.

which unfolded the events immediately to precede the coming of the millennial kingdom, he presented a striking contrast between the emerging age of peace and the despicable system of British corruption patterned after the practices of Sir Robert Walpole. Before passing on to the more pleasant scenes of millennial bliss, Dwight paused to examine at length the substance and origins of British corruption, and his thoughts clarify an important assumption of his and his colleagues' political analysis. The overt system of British corruption and tyranny, he insisted, reflected the "public operation" of "the infernal principle of selfishness" which had infected the nation. That the prime minister could "ensure him a vote for every purpose" or that American rights were flagrantly violated by the British Parliament indicated that "the fountain of wicked actions" had finally spilled over into public as well as private life, thereby "reducing wickedness to a system." With only a glance at the outward appearance of British politics, Dwight probed the heart of the matter and identified that spring of immoral action which had poisoned the whole of Britain's national character, leaving no sector untainted.[17]

Dwight's emphasis on the moral foundations of tyranny represents a particular shading of republican thought that New Englanders had expressed thoughout the Revolution. Never far beneath the dramatic fears of sword and shackle lay the quiet dread that Britain's moral disease might spread to the New World. Reflecting on the Declaration of Independence in 1780, Nathan Strong cheered the separation not only because it squelched the "arts of a corrupt court" but also for another reason. As he put it: "Had the national connection continued longer, a familiar intercourse would have introduced into this

---

17. Timothy Dwight, *A Sermon Preached at Northampton* . . . (Hartford, 1781), pp. 14–29, quotations on pp. 18, 29, 17, 14.

new country that declension of morals, which hath usually been produced in an old empire . . . ."[18] In concen-
trating on vice as the root of tyranny, New England
certainly did not differ in kind from other Americans
schooled in radical Whiggery, but neither was their focus
on the "minds, habits, and morals of a people"[19] a precise
transcript of other republican anxieties fueled primarily
by banks, merchants, speculators, stockjobbers, and
standing armies. Was the bitter taste of tyranny the worst
evil to be feared, or did it only foreshadow the more
awesome poison of moral bankruptcy? The end of war
and the removal of the heavy-handed threat of foreign
tyranny brought this question to mind in different form,
one which would accentuate the differences in the already
contrasting dialects of republicanism.

New England ministers did not find much in Thomas
Paine's *The Rights of Man* that escaped their hostility,
but upon one point they were in full agreement with
Paine; namely, that "What is called a *republic,* is not any
particular form of government."[20] Like any American
immersed in the Commonwealth tradition, they were
firmly convinced that the "foundation of every government is some principle or passion in the minds of the
people."[21] It was this active spring of conduct, this disposition of national character, which gave rise to those
forms of government notable for their liberty. The foundation of the American Republic, moreover, heightened
the patriots' concern for that inner principle of republican freedom. While a benevolent monarch might be able

18. Nathan Strong, *The Agency and Providence of God Acknowledged . . .* (Hartford, 1780), pp. 12–13.
19. Samuel Williams, *The Influence of Christianity on Civil Society . . .* (Boston, 1780), p. 8.
20. Thomas Paine, *The Rights of Man* (London, 1791), *The Complete Writings of Thomas Paine,* ed. Philip S. Foner (New York, 1945), 1:369.
21. John Adams, *Thoughts on Government,* in *The Works of John Adams,* ed. Charles Francis Adams, 4 (Boston, 1851), 194.

to control a society bereft of virtue, in a republic the full responsibility for liberty reverted to the people. "Virtue is the spirit of a Republic; for where all power is derived from the people, all depends on their good disposition."[22]

In describing the relationship between virtue and liberty, Americans in the 1780s referred most often to examples of classical Greece and Rome. The didactic lessons of the ancient world, however, were hardly encouraging for the new nation. Not only were "Republics, in their very constitution . . . shorter lifed than other governments," but when one inquired "on what rocks" these states had "split and dashed to pieces," the historical record made it emphatically clear: their own vice and decay were responsible, not foreign conquest.[23] With the dark recognition that no republican state had ever flourished without being corrupted from within, Americans were forced to crush the traitorous spirit of vice in every form.

The quest for political virtue thus became the preeminent responsibility of American patriots. Projecting the model citizen of the classical republics, they defined virtue in terms of martial spirit, industry, honesty, frugality, and most importantly, that disinterestedness which demanded that all must give way to the public good. It was these "rustic traits of the sturdy yeoman" in which Americans placed their frail yet determined hope. The classical citizen, both honorable and humble, virile and benevolent, served as the personification of what the American hoped he would become.[24]

It was, then, a voice in the wilderness which pro-

22. Samuel Cooper, *A Sermon Preached before His Excellency John Hancock* . . . (Boston, 1780), p. 37; Wood, *The Creation of the American Republic,* pp. 65–70.

23. David Tappan, *The Question Answered* . . . (Salem, 1783), p. 13.

24. Wood, *The Creation of the American Republic,* pp. 48–53, quotation on p. 52.

claimed that one of the first political errors of the new republic was "too high a respect for the state of society in Greece and Rome." This opinion of Timothy Dwight, Yale's new president and increasingly a prophet not to be understood south of Connecticut, attacked not the ideals of the ancient republics, but the inability of Greece and Rome to "give stability to their respective political systems."[25] According to Dwight's analysis, the sincere energies of the classical republican citizen had been misdirected in means that could never accomplish his worthy goals. While they were preoccupied with political matters—the constructing of "numerous checks, balances, and divisions of power and influence"—and their respective nations as a result became giants in war, science, art, and government, citizens of classical Greece and Rome maintained a deficient working definition of virtue. In assuming too quickly the sufficiency of their own national character, they had failed to comprehend the depths of their own moral problem, thereby taking pride in that which would shortly become their Achilles' heel.[26]

In Dwight's mind the classical definition of virtue was bankrupt even before the premature demise of those republics which embodied it. The sages of the ancient world, confident of the state's political strength, had failed to develop a "plan of amending the human character." Never contributing anything more than "accidental improvements" to the national moral fiber, the Greeks and Romans remained infants in the development of virtue, unable to control those forces which predisposed men to be "ignorant, vicious, and unhappy . . . slaves of appetite and passion."[27] Dwight's disillusionment with

25. Timothy Dwight, *The True Means of Establishing Public Happiness* . . . (New Haven, Conn., 1795), pp. 11–12, 5–6.
26. Ibid., pp. 6, 9–10.
27. Ibid., pp. 11, 12, 9, 12.

even the best of the classical world vividly depicts that definition of virtue which gave New England republican thought its distinct moral ring. Classical virtue failed to measure up to the standards of the strenuous Yankees.

These stern moralists were not always comforted when fellow citizens spoke of the importance of virtue; with Dwight, they despised the kind of political excellence which never delved below the surface of human political, social, and economic relationships.[28] Although they did find time to discuss such crucial issues as the importance of the freehold, the danger of commerce, and the need for a militia, they were convinced that these were incidental. The more crucial question, upon which the republic would rise or fall, burned in their minds throughout the Critical Period. It ran along these lines: "But can the selfishness of the heart be tamed? Can cords bind this Leviathan so as not to be broken asunder?"[29] The highly libertarian political structure of the new nation failed to allay these fears because the question returned to haunt them in more devastating form: "Is human nature essentially different in this new world, from what it ever has been and still is in the old?" Unless the nation wished to build on a foundation of sand, it had to face the stark reality that "human depravity is the life and the soul of slavery."[30]

New England ministers would have had no quarrel with Thomas Jefferson's suggestion in 1780 that those who labor in the earth had been set apart by God for a special role in the republic. But when he went on to say that "*Corruption* of morals in the mass of cultivators is a phenomenon of which no age nor nation has furnished an

28. Asa Burton, *A Sermon Preached at Windsor, before His Excellency Thomas Chittenden* . . . (Windsor, Vt., 1786), p. 22.

29. Ibid., p. 13.

30. Tappan, *The Question Answered,* p. 14; Samuel Miller, *A Sermon Preached in New-York* . . . (New York, 1793), p. 13.

example," they would have gaped in startled disbelief.[31] As crucial as a man's land-based independence was for the social order, the idea that a man was endowed with virtue by reason of his social and economic condition was a theorem without foundation, a principle easily disproved by Scripture, history, and experience. What could a freehold do to tame the basic restlessness, the unruly passions, the dissolute spirit which all men, farmers and urban citizens alike, held in common? With men everywhere driven by "an avaritious selfish spirit," bursting "the bonds of moral obligation," and promoting "strife and vexious discord," the sermons of the 1780s had as their dominant theme the necessity for the republic to restrain, check, and control rebellious human nature.[32] Unconvinced that America's rural character alleviated its predicament in any significant way, New England ministers saw pitfalls all along the road to political virtue. Prospects for the United States were, as David Tappan concluded in 1783, anything but bright:

I shall therefore endeavour to show, that though the morning of our political deliverance is come, yet a dark night in some respects still overspreads us, and a darker still seems preparing to visit us; which threatens to eclipse, if not totally extinguish, that dawning light, which has begun to cheer and bless this western world. . . . Which leads me to add, the common depravity of human nature, in which we share with the rest of our species, casts a dark shade over the present bright interval, and too strongly presages that it will not be constant and lasting. Such is the depraved temper of our fallen world.[33]

In defining republican virtue, the clergy had to begin with those wells of vice which made their impact on

31. Thomas Jefferson, *Notes on the State of Virginia,* ed. William Peden (Chapel Hill, N. C., 1955), pp. 164–65.
32. Henry Cumings, *A Sermon Preached in Billerica* . . . (Boston, 1784), p. 36.
33. Tappan, *The Question Answered,* pp. 12–13.

political as well as other forms of behavior. And given this presupposition, simple definitions of virtue such as "the Love of doing good" or "mental energy, directed steadily to that which is right"[34] became laden with a complex set of assumptions drawn from the deep tradition of New England's shared social and religious experience. Driven by the compulsion to preserve the fragile republic, ministers found no other hope but to return to a heritage which had long sustained God's New English Israel. Amazingly contemporary and anachronistic at the same time, they sought to build republican liberty upon a foundation far more Hebraic and Puritan than classical and humanist. They understood virtue and its three supporting pillars "in that enlarged and Evangelical sense, which embraces Piety to God, Good-will to mankind, and the effectual Government of ourselves."[35]

During the Revolution ministers delighted in sermon texts which dealt with Israel's struggle for liberty against Pharoah, and in celebrations of victory throughout the 1780s they likewise spoke repeatedly of Moses leading the people out of Egyptian bondage. But as in the experience of that analogue to General Washington, grumbling and discontent soon muffled the song of victory and church members in the new nation heard stern warnings such as Reverend Charles Turner gave to students at Harvard in 1783: "Remember the case of those, *whose carcases* [sic] *fell in the wilderness;* those *murmurers,* who despised the promised land, and desired to return to Egypt."[36] The picture of a greatly blessed people, who in spite of the "furnace of afflictive discipline" continued

34. Dwight, *The True Means,* p. 14.
35. Ibid., p. 13.
36. Charles Turner, *Due Glory to be Given to God* . . . (Boston, 1783), p. 18. A member of the State Senate at the time, Turner's chief exhortation to the students was to excel "in love to God and their country; in truly christian, and republican sobriety" (pp. 30–31).

their dissatisfaction, convinced the clergy that real virtue was impossible without a firm commitment to Christian piety—in the words of the type, without the concurrent agency of Aaron as well as Moses.[37]

Political virtue without a sincere fear of God posed a serious contradiction in terms. "Virtue and piety are nearly connected—married by heaven," declared the theological maverick John Murray in 1779, "no man can divide them—where impiety reigns virtue is banished and when she takes her departure the community has lost the surest guardian of public safety."[38] This widely shared conclusion, pointing in the direction of a Christian republic, followed two lines of argument. In the first place, it was asserted that nothing less than a belief in God's moral government and the approaching state of reward and punishment would effectively check the unruly passion of men. "Having got beyond the restraints of a divine authority, they will not brook the control of laws enacted by rulers of their own creating."[39] While law could only punish criminal actions, religion could "tear up the roots from which they grow." The Christian religion could redirect the very source of human conduct and thus form better citizens in all walks of life. New Englanders were convinced that while others could speculate about liberty, they could find "the true patriot only in the true christian."[40]

37. Ibid., p. 13; David Tappan, *A Sermon Preached before His Excellency John Hancock* . . . (Boston, 1792), p. 6.

38. John Murray, *Nehemiah, or the Struggle for Liberty Never in Vain* (Newburyport, Mass., 1779), p. 44.

39. Cooper, *A Sermon Preached before His Excellency John Hancock*, p. 37; Dwight, *The True Means of Establishing Public Happiness*, p. 21.

40. Tappan, *A Sermon Preached before His Excellency John Hancock*, p. 11; John Cosens Ogden, *A Sermon Delivered before His Excellency the President* . . . (Concord, N. H., 1790), p. 3. The Presbyterian Samuel Miller devoted an entire sermon to the Christian basis of liberty: "The truth is, that political liberty does not rest, solely, on the form of government, under which a nation may happen to live. . . . Human laws are too imperfect in themselves, to

This emphasis on the civic necessity of personal subjection to the laws of God was fueled by another equally
traditional mode of understanding, the vision of society
as a body politic. Individual impiety was certainly serious
enough, but these corporate assumptions made any disease contagious to the whole. There was no such thing as
private sin; even such faults as swearing, blasphemy, and
idleness were considered "diseases of the political body,
which prey upon its very vitals, and by certain, tho'
insensible degrees, bring on its dissolution."[41] Given the
fact that the whole community would suffer by the mis-
conduct of the individual, religion took on even greater
importance. What other remedy could aid the political
body when "rack'd with malignant disorders which sur-
pass the *political physician's* skill to heal or remedy?" For
New Englanders the republican dictum making a virtuous nation and a vicious individual an "inadmissible
solecism in ethics" became even more highly charged.
Even the meditations of the heart became potential
"Tumors in the Body-politic."[42]

These deeply felt corporate assumptions, certainly of
the vibrant hues of Puritanism the slowest to fade with
time, were expressed most intensely when ministers
spoke of their second expectation of the virtuous citizen,

secure completely this inestimable blessing. It must have its seat in the hearts
and dispositions of those individuals which compose the body politic; and it is
with the hearts and dispositions of men that Christianity is conversant. When,
therefore, that *perfect law of liberty*, which this holy religion includes, prevails
and governs in the minds of all, their freedom rests upon a basis more solid and
immoveable, than human wisdom can devise." See *Christianity the Grand
Source, and the Surest Basis, of Political Liberty* (New York, 1793), pp. 13–14.

41. Samuel Macclintock, *A Sermon Preached before the Honorable the
Council* (Portsmouth, N. H., 1784), pp. 34–35.

42. Jonas Clarke, *A Sermon Preached before His Excellency John Hancock . . .* (Boston, 1781), p. 15; Dan Foster, *An Election Sermon Before the
Honorable Legislature* (Windsor, Vt., 1790), p. 23; Turner, *Due Glory to be
Given to God,* p. 33; Nathan Williams, *A Sermon Preached in the Audience of
the General Assembly . . .* (Hartford, 1780), p. 10.

his personal responsibility for the public good. "When every man regards the welfare of his brother and of the whole, the political body is strong, full of energy and happiness."[43] This ideal of commonwealth, grounded in individual sacrifice for the public good, became on one level a shared assumption of most postwar political literature. Throughout America the fact of having toppled a government which served the interest of despot and courtier fired hopes that in the New World an authentic commonwealth might arise, one which promoted *res publica* as the sole end of government. Beyond this ubiquitous republican goal, however, New Englanders expressed a shading of thought setting them noticeably apart from others who shared the concern that government "ought to be, calculated for the general good and safety of the community."[44] Rejecting outright the notion that tyranny would vanish when government came to rest on the consent of the people, clergymen wrestled instead with the herculean task of eradicating selfishness, "the fountain of wicked actions." "Mankind are divided into two classes," said Asa Burton, "by two very opposite principles, those of selfishness and benevolence. From these result the different practices, fruits, and characters, which distinguish those classes from each other."[45] Convinced that the only basis of a free republic was benevolence, a man's solid conviction that "he was born, not for himself alone, but for others, for society, for his country,"[46] the clergy found little cause for joy in their moral examination of the body politic. Unlike many of their

43. Nathan Strong, *A Sermon Delivered in the Presence of His Excellency Samuel Huntington* . . . (Hartford, 1790), p. 13.

44. Wood, *The Origins of the American Republic,* p. 55.

45. Dwight, *A Sermon Preached at Northampton,* p. 14; Burton, *A Sermon Preached at Windsor,* p. 5.

46. Henry Cumings, *A Sermon Preached before His Honor Thomas Cushing* . . . (Boston, 1783), p. 8.

fellow patriots, who might equate the public good with a government of common consent, assuming that "the bulk of the people, both mean and think right,"[47] New Englanders would not accept simple answers to what they defined as complex questions. They feared most not the flagrant violator of the public good, but the patriot who would contribute to the welfare of the whole with "external diligence and activity,"[48] and would perform such duties out of motives of self-interest. By resisting the temptation to accept as the basis of a free state anything less than a complete change of moral character from selfishness to benevolence, clergymen maintained faith with a beautiful dream, but ran the risk of having it suddenly turn into a nightmare.

At no time during the 1780s did the pastors of New England overcome their besetting anxiety that their republican dream would, in the words of John Adam's cousin, Zabdiel, "vanish like the baseless fabrick of a vision."[49] Knowing well the lessons of history that vice and virtue were "the great hinges on which the fates of nations turn," they evaluated the characteristic impiety and selfishness of their fellow countrymen and concluded that "this new empire will not be of long duration, at least in its present form, unless they are restrained by some effectual expedients." It was to this problem that they addressed themselves in defining the third dimension of virtue, what Timothy Dwight called "the effectual Government of ourselves."[50]

47. Wood, *The Origins of the American Republic*, p. 56.
48. Samuel Austin, *Disinterested Love the Ornament of the Christian* (New York, 1791), p. 30.
49. Zabdiel Adams, *A Sermon Preached before His Excellency . . .* (Boston, 1782), p. 48.
50. William Symmes, *A Sermon Preached before His Honor Thomas Cushing . . .* (Boston, 1785), p. 5; Macclintock, *A Sermon Preached before the Honorable Council*, pp. 34–35; Dwight, *The True Means of Establishing Public Happiness*, p. 13.

If the "contagion of liberty"[51] infected New England clergymen during the closing years of the American Revolution, it had little success in moving men in the direction of democracy. Far from propelling Congregational ministers into modernity, the prospect of a free republic evoked a decidedly reactionary pattern of thought, one which called upon the individual to govern himself by the premodern criteria of inequality, deference, subordination, and authority. Fearful that members of society would at any moment fly off from "the public good . . . the attracting point, the common centre of gravity," and take "an eccentric course," ministers constantly appealed for men to "conform to the great law of mutual subjection" and to "pay strict attention to the natural aristocracy, which is the institution of heaven."[52] Calling for the citizen to demonstrate "faithfulness in his station," the pulpit echoed with Pauline texts which distinguished between gold and wood, strong and weak, head and "uncomely parts."[53] "Men, who are said to be born in a state of equality, are yet endowed with unequal measures of strength and wisdom," suggested Joseph Lyman to a Boston audience in 1787. "To affirm that in the qualifications to rule and guide, all men are equal, is

51. Bernard Bailyn has argued that the American Revolution unleashed a flood of pragmatic idealism which swept established social assumptions and institutions into the past and thrust the new nation toward romantic democracy. While in New England this contagion of liberty did increase the clergy's opposition to chattel slavery, it did little to break down clerical hostility to democratic ideas or to dissuade them from the belief that the republic should be distinctively Christian. See chap. 6, "The Contagion of Liberty," in *The Ideological Origins of the American Revolution* (Cambridge, Mass., 1967), pp. 230–319.

52. Cumings, *A Sermon Preached before His Honor Thomas Cushing*, pp. 15, 7; Elizur Goodrich, *The Principles of Civil Union and Happiness Considered and Recommended* . . . (Hartford, 1787), p. 20.

53. James Dana, *A Sermon Preached before the General Assembly* . . . (Hartford, 1779), p. 7; Joseph Huntington, *A Discourse* . . . *on the Health and Happiness or Misery and Ruin of the Body Politic in Similitude to that of the Natural Body* (Hartford, 1781), pp. 3–6.

to blend characters totally diverse, to confound wisdom with folly, and affability and condescension with ill-nature and pride."[54] With a mental fixation on the image of a body politic, all knew that "every member must keep their respective places or it becomes a hideous and a horrid monster."[55]

Within the context of these expectations, which sought an ordered society of voluntary restraint, clergymen cast about for more predictable methods of controlling vice. History and experience offered only one clear solution, a tight bond between the civil and sacred orders. "One thing is clear," affirmed William Symmes of Andover in the Massachusetts Election Sermon of 1785, "that a constitution of government, that bids fair to be durable, must make provision for curbing the lusts, and bounding the riotous appetites of men."[56] Resisting any attempt to divest the civil government of its spiritual responsibility, ministers looked to the authorities of the republic as the primary deterrent to those evil energies about to catapult the new nation into chaos. The depths of the republic's moral problem intensified the clergy's confidence in civil officers as guardians of the public safety. According to John Murray,

the security of the body is the government's charge—that can never be had where the reins are laid on the necks of men's lusts, and immoralities are under no public restraint—the system of laws that affixes no penalty to theft, adultery, murder, and the like enormities, is justly regarded as designedly opening the widest door for undoing the State: nor is it easy to say why those should be punished whilst blasphemy and profaning the name of God—whilst public mockery of his word, his day and his worship, enjoy the sanction of a public license;

---

54. Joseph Lyman, *A Sermon Preached before His Excellency James Bowdoin* . . . (Boston, 1787), p. 8.
55. Huntingdon, *A Discourse* . . . *on the Health and Happiness*, p. 23.
56. Symmes, *A Sermon Preached before His Honor Thomas Cushing*, p. 16.

and for ought that appears, may plead the shelter of legal establishment. It is hard to investigate any ingredient in the acts restrained
more truly pernicious, than is the whole nature of those that go free,
unless we conclude that the first table of God's law is not as binding
and authoritative as the second—or that obedience to the one excul-
pates the breacher of the other, or that killing the body is a greater
crime than destroying the soul; or in a word, that every member may
be ruined and the community safe.[57]

In addition to relentless advice that civil authorities
should suppress public and personal vice, clergymen also
entrusted elected leaders with the "two great means
of promoting virtue; Religious Education and Public
Worship."[58] The preservation of free government was
contingent upon a society's investment in "Christian and
republican education" as well as in the strict regulation of
church attendance, where the impact of religion might
regularly inflame the heart with pure affection.[59]

By thus elevating civil authorities as the true "Ministers
of God for good to his people,"[60] the clergy continued a
long-standing tradition of assigning the magistrate qual-
ities of moral wisdom and disinterested oversight of the
public good. With remarkable consistency, the more
New Englanders were repelled by moral decadence, the
more they became attracted to the kind of leadership
which their ancestors had described as a speaking aristoc-

57. Murray, *Nehemiah or the Struggle for Liberty,* pp. 44–45.
58. Dwight, *The True Means of Establishing Public Happiness,* p. 35.
59. Macclintock, *A Sermon Preached before the Honorable Council,* p. 37;
Turner, *Due Glory to be Given to God,* p. 30; Clarke, *A Sermon Preached
before His Excellency John Hancock,* p. 37. That the clergy argued so sincerely
and with such deep conviction to preserve their own social role is an excellent
illustration of Peter Berger's analysis of ideology: "Deliberate deception requires a degree of psychological self-control that few people are capable of.
That is why insincerity is rather a rare phenomenon. Most people are sincere,
because this is the easiest course to take psychologically. . . . ideology both
justifies what is done by the group whose vested interest is served and interprets
social reality in such a way that the justification is made plausible" (Berger,
Invitation to Sociology: A Humanistic Perspective [Garden City, N. Y., 1963],
pp. 109, 112).
60. Dwight, *Virtuous Rulers a National Blessing,* p. 33.

racy in the face of a silent democracy. The perceptions of Timothy Dwight are an almost unbroken theme in sermons throughout the Critical Period:

> Perhaps no country has enjoyed the government of so many rulers, of distinguished virtue, as this. Our rulers have not only been decent, and unexceptionable, but bold, strenuous and exemplary, in their virtue.
> ... A ruler is here the favourite object of the approbation, and the choice, of an immense number of wise and good men. He is singled out from other men, not by conquest, law, or birth, but by the hearts of those, who obey.[61]

With a deep conviction that rulers were men of "superior abilities," an aristocracy "founded in merit and designed by the God of government and order," the clergy called upon them to serve as an effectual guard against anarchy and confusion: "Honour and respect are due to rulers:" insisted Elizur Goodrich of Durham, Connecticut, "the order and good of society require external marks of distinction, and titles of eminence to be given them."[62] In this recognition of the magistrate's moral superiority, the absence of clerical fears that rulers would degenerate into tyrants is as remarkable as the common assumption that subjects would "abuse their privileges, and become disorderly, ungovernable, undutiful, factious, and irreligious."[63] Having avoided the Charybdis of despotic tyranny with victory over Britain, the clergy of New England approached the decade of peace which followed convinced that unavoidable currents of disorder and anarchy were sweeping the frail republican ship towards the rocks of Scylla. Their demand for rulers of moral strength may have foreshadowed the tumult and confusion which plagued

61. Ibid., pp. 28–29, 35.
62. Goodrich, *The Principles of Civil Union and Happiness,* pp. 20–21, 22–24.
63. Hemmenway, *A Sermon Preached before His Excellency John Hancock,* p. 32.

New England after 1789, but its deepest roots were in their analysis of the moral deficiencies of the republic.

℥

Reflecting on the condition of America in 1783, Charles Turner described the fledgling republic as a "figure of *a man* who is industrious, as soon and as fast as possible, to destroy with one hand, that which he is most earnestly contending to build up with the other."[64] This image, and numerous others which suggested a split personality in the body politic, became a primary motif in New England during these years. The victory over Britain, on the one hand, formed America as "the permanent seat of Liberty" and thus became "a principal link" in that chain which hastened the fulfillment of the millennium. "And as the flame of Liberty burns brighter in America," spoke a confident Levi Frisbie, minister at Ipswich, " . . . will not our example and our intercourse with foreign nations widely diffuse this sacred flame, and extend its happy influence thro' all the Kingdoms of Europe, if not to the most distant quarters of the globe?"[65] It was this style of exultant rhetoric which led Perry Miller to place victorious New England "on a pinnacle of virtuousness," the military victory having fulfilled its definition of social regeneration. Leaving behind "the exciting scenes both of war and spiritual conflict," the clergy in Miller's scheme "headed for a monotonous, and uninteresting prosperity, the flatness of universal virtue."[66]

64. Turner, *Due Glory to be Given to God,* p. 17.
65. David Tappan, *A Discourse Delivered at the Third Parish in Newbury* . . . (Salem, 1783), p. 12; Adams, *A Sermon Preached before His Excellency John Hancock,* p. 57; Levi Frisbie, *An Oration Delivered at Ipswich* . . . (Boston, 1783), pp. 15–16.
66. Perry Miller, "From the Covenant to the Revival," in *The Shaping of American Religion,* ed. J. W. Smith and A. L. Jamison (Princeton, N. J., 1961), pp. 343–44, 349.

Focusing precisely on this sense of attainment and expectation, Miller presents an undistorted picture of the clergy's mood—as far as he goes. But a more comprehensive view, while not diminishing the lofty optimism which he notes, must somehow explain the equally extreme valleys of despair, the intensified theme of jeremiad evoked by the need for republican virtue. The paradoxical legacy of the Revolution left New Englanders in a state of dizzying mental fluctuation. If the war set ablaze the flame of liberty, the primary external manifestation of a republic, the eight years of conflict also seemed to extinguish that virtue which was the heart and soul of free states. Two weeks after David Tappan of Newburg celebrated the peace treaty with euphoric anticipation that recent events would "wake up and encourage the dormant flame of liberty in all quarters of the earth," and hasten "the accomplishment of the scripture-prophecies relative to the *Millennial State*,"[67] he spoke with categorical pessimism about the moral ramifications of the victory:

If this then has been the state and progress of things, while we have been under the fettors and terrors of war, what are we to expect, now these restraints are taken off, and our unsubdued lusts permitted to range and riot at large among the tempting sweets of a fertile, peaceful country, and to call in to their entertainment the delicacies and luxuries of all foreign climes?[68]

The continuing interplay between republican liberty and a particular New England definition of virtue provides not only the basic index of clerical thought during the 1780s, but also, and more importantly, the key to understanding how near-paranoid cries for liberty in the

67. Tappan, *A Discourse Delivered at the Third Parish in Newbury*, p. 12. In 1792 Tappan was named Hollis Professor of Divinity at Harvard.
68. Tappan, *The Question Answered*, p. 15.

1770s became equally intense demands for order by the 1790s. During the Revolution those energies of the opposition tradition which had given birth to republican ideals were directed to tearing down the awesome image of tyranny and found little time or reason to predict the moral readiness of America for republican institutions. The struggle against tyranny accentuated both the moral deficiencies of Britain and America's sense of devotion to a common and virtuous cause.

During the Critical Period, however, as patriots could no longer defend the cause of liberty with musket and sword, the pressure to sustain a government of liberty created a stern mood of collective introspection, steeled by the conviction that the present moment is "the crisis of our fate—the great season of our national probation."[69] Having watched the divine wonders against "Pharoah" and having quickly taken up arms to overthrow "Egypt," New Englanders knew that their perilous experiment, now in the wilderness, depended on nothing but their own moral fitness. While continuing to adhere to those republican goals, shared by Americans from Georgia to New Hampshire, New Englanders demanded, in their own distinct way, the renewal of the inner man of the body politic.

Their dialect of republicanism, heavy with ethical overtones, often reflected perceptions of the republic as commonwealth, virtue as piety and benevolence, vice as sin, and liberty as opportunity to do what is right. Even specific political principles such as the balance of power were often altered to imply a moral lesson, in this case, "that all the members should know their place, and the duties of their station, in the Commonwealth, whether in

69. Ibid., p. 18.

authority, or subordination."[70] It is this cast of mind which foreshadowed the threats of anarchy, discord, faction, and infidelity which Shays's Rebellion seemed to unleash in 1787 and which, for that generation, would seem to have no end.[71] In a real sense the prophecies of doom early in the Critical Period were no less self-fulfilling than warnings regarding the insatiable goals of tyranny a decade earlier. In both cases, a pattern of expectations gave definition to specific political contexts and thereby charted the various political options available to the New England patriot.

During the 1790s, New England's political elite clearly endowed the crisis-torn political world with meanings drawn from their past. The clergy's evaluation of the administrations of both Washington and Adams and of the motives and methods of the Democratic Republicans reflects values hammered out during the postwar period of their demand for a republic of Christian virtue. The feeling that the world was splitting apart at the seams did have a most profound and agonizing effect upon New England thought, a convulsion not to be underestimated, but like Paul Revere's tidings two decades earlier, the alterations created in the mental landscape accentuated patterns already there.

70. Jonas Clarke, *A Sermon Preached before His Excellency John Hancock,* p. 31. Intimate friend of Boston radicals, Clarke knew nothing of subordination in April of 1775, when Paul Revere's famous announcement sent Samuel Adams and John Hancock scurrying from his Lexington parsonage. Later, Parson Clarke wildly exaggerated British atrocities at the battle of Lexington in a sermon *Fate of the Blood-Thirsty Oppressors* . . . (Boston, 1776).

71. Shays's Rebellion intensified the clergy's entrenched fear of "savage independence" and "the riotous appetites of men." Compare Jeremy Belknap, *An Election Sermon Preached before the General Court of New-Hampshire* . . . (Portsmouth, N. H., 1785), p. 18 and William Symmes, *A Sermon Preached before His Honor Thomas Cushing* . . . (Boston, 1785), p. 16 with Josiah Whitney's response to the uprising, *The Essential Requisites to Form the Good Rulers Character* . . . (New Haven, 1788), p. 36.

During the 1790s Yankee ministers came to idealize the republican form of government under which they lived much as their fathers had idealized the British constitution. In contrast to their discontent with the counselors of the first chief executive and the counsel of the second, Yankee Congregationalists insisted that their national officials were "unrivalled by any other set of rulers in any other nation under the sun." "Under almost every other government," said David Osgood of Medford, Massachusetts, "the people have some real grievance of which to complain; but in this good land, there are no such grounds for complaint or disquietude. The inhabitants are the freest and happiest in the world."[72] The clergy's pictures of American government pointing the world in a millennial direction reflected the sincere conviction that in the New World forms of government in fact approximated republican ideals.

The reason for this was simple enough: political institutions in America embodied that ideal of liberty for which men had risked their lives in battle and through which the history of mankind would soon draw to a triumphant close. But an increasing number of Americans, in New England and elsewhere, reckoned that Federalist liberty had the same bent as the freedom promised by King George; drawing upon the well-stocked arsenal of opposition argument, they attacked corruption, arbitrary power, and the influence of monied interests in the new government.[73] Against these charges

72. David Osgood, *Some Facts Evincive . . .* (Boston, 1798), p. 23. Osgood's parishioners with sympathies for Jefferson did have real grievances of which to complain. More than any of his colleagues, Osgood used the pulpit to berate his political opponents, some of whom, it is said, would actually exit while he was preaching. See Clifford K. Shipton, *Sibley's Harvard Graduates,* vol. 17 (Boston, 1975), pp. 570–80.
73. For a comprehensive study of Democratic-Republican thought, see Lance G. Banning, "The Quarrel with Federalism: A Study in the Origins and Character of Republican Thought" (Ph.D. diss., Washington University, 1971).

Congregational ministers built a defense around the idea of balanced liberty, arguing that the first two American presidents had preserved liberty "from *aristocratic* and *democratic* tyranny."[74] Henry Cumings of Billerica, who three decades earlier worried that a "Frenchified party" had come to power in Britain, now boasted, in 1797, that the United States avoided the errors of both European powers:

The civil constitutions of government under which we live are poised, in an even balance, between the extremes of arbitrary power and despotism, on the one hand, and of anarchy and unrestrained licentiousness, on the other; and are evidently founded on as broad a basis of liberty, as can consist with the end and design of social compacts.[75]

On either side of their own "happy union of liberty and order,"[76] New Englanders saw nations gripped by one form of tyranny or the other. Under a pretense of republican liberty, France had merely substituted a more insidious tyranny. "The same crimes have stained their character when professing liberty and equality as when sounding the praises of their kings," suggested Jeremy Belknap, "and their national character, instead of being meliorated, is, if possible, degenerated by their revolutions; for slaves, when made free, are the worst of tyrants."[77] While rejecting outright this "savage independence" of the French, the pastors of New England did not, as their critics charged, suddenly leap into the secure arms of Britain's ancient constitution. Although they knew full well "which is the weakest side of our

74. Ezra Weld, *A Discourse, Delivered April 25, 1799* ... (Boston, 1799), p. 14.

75. Henry Cumings, *A Sermon Preached at Billerica, December 15, 1796* ... (Boston, 1797), p. 16. For the earlier sermon, given during the Stamp Act crisis, see page 84 above.

76. David Tappan, *Christian Thankfulness* ...(Boston, 1795), p. 20.

77. Jeremy Belknap, *A Sermon Delivered on the 9th of May, 1798* (Boston, 1798), p. 17.

government" and that they had to guard more emphatically against democracy and leveling,[78] they insisted that they had not reneged on libertarian principle. "If there be any persons among us who are for re-uniting us, with Great Britain," warned Belknap in 1798, "I hold their political principles in as much abhorrence as those who are for subjecting us to the influence of France." The idea of monarchy and "elevating certain families, and securing to their descendants the power and rank of kings and nobles" had no more appeal for these republicans than the thought of every man becoming a law unto himself.[79] God's new Israel, so the argument went, should enjoy the balanced liberty of the Promised Land without "hankering after the leeks and onions of Egypt" or exalting that wilderness generation which sought freedom from all legal obligation.[80]

The political import of this idealization of the actual structure of American government is striking, as evidenced by the centripetal effect of such incidents as the Whiskey Rebellion.[81] Convinced that "opposition to the laws, in a free government, is a crime which liberty cannot tolerate,"[82] ministers seemed unable to discuss the specific grievances of Pennsylvania farmers because of their own preoccupation with the morality of the case. Given the premise that President Washington's "wise and liberal government" was characterized by exemplary un-

78. Jeremy Belknap, *An Election Sermon Preached before the General Court* (Portsmouth, N. H., 1785), p. 18; Nathaniel Emmons, *A Discourse Delivered May 9, 1798* (Wrentham, Conn., 1798), p. 22.

79. Belknap, *A Sermon Delivered on the 9th of May, 1798*, p. 19; Henry Channing, *The Consideration of Divine Goodness* ... (New London, Conn., 1794), p. 18.

80. John Cushing, *A Discourse Delivered at Ashburnham* ... (Leominster, Mass., 1796), p. 19.

81. Leland D. Baldwin, *Whiskey Rebels: The Story of a Frontier Uprising* (Pittsburgh, Pa., 1939).

82. Channing, *The Consideration of Divine Goodness*, p. 21.

derstanding and firmness, what other conclusion could be drawn than that dissidents were "deluded insurgents" driven by the "impulse of unlimited, disappointed avarice, ambition, or vanity, or from the malignant feelings of envy and party animosity"?[83] Appalled that the rebels treated the officials of government with a boldness and indignity "which a man would hardly use towards a servant in his family," Levi Frisbie could only surmise that his countrymen needed strong teaching on "the sacred nature of civil Government, and the sacred character of its ministers."[84] Opposition to Federalist policy, in this and many subsequent cases, only brought into precise focus what he and his colleagues in the pulpit had already perceived from afar.

From their very first glimpse of the envisioned American republic, the Standing Order of New England had been anxious lest liberty should crumble into licentiousness and lest men, heady with the removal of certain strictures, should struggle to "get free from all legal obligations."[85] Despite their fifteen-year confrontation with tyranny of an aristocratic sort, ministers in 1780 had called for a balanced freedom which, curiously enough, threw all the weight of restraint against the threat of anarchy. Taking seriously the dictum that the primary purpose of government was to restrain the corruptions of human nature, ministers reconsecrated the magistrate as God's minister for good and called repeatedly for the expansion of his legal and moral authority. The overwhelming support of the Congregational establishment for the adoption of the new constitution, as James Smylie

83. Levi Frisbie, *A Sermon Delivered February 19, 1795* (Newburyport, Mass., 1795), p. 18; Tappan, *Christian Thankfulness*, p. 21.

84. Frisbie, *A Sermon Delivered February 19, 1795*, p. 23.

85. Samuel Langdon, *The Republic of the Israelites an Example to the American States* (Exeter, N. H., 1788), pp. 47–48.

has demonstrated, is another evidence of the predisposition to encourage a kind of republican law and order.[86]

Early in the Critical Period these defenders of established authority grouped their forces around that point at which the republic seemed most vulnerable: ministers fully expected flattering politicians to take advantage of the ignorant and unprincipled. They were extremely wary that Americans would be "seduced into a surrender of their liberties, by the specious acts, eloquence and address of designing men, whose enterprising ambition will not fail to lay hold on such an advantage." The dissolute spirit which seemed to possess the body of the people marked them as "easy prey for ambitious power." It was assumed that aspiring politicians would plant the seeds of faction, the firstfruits, as it were, "of envy and disappointed ambition."[87] This would, in turn, break down confidence in government, unleash faction and party strife, and, worst of all, set in motion a process of irreversible decline: when this "convulsive disease" had entered a state "it unstrings the nerves of government, and introduces such disorder and uncertainty into public measures, and such strife and division among people, as are inconsistent with the public safety, security and prosperity."[88] The strategy of the clergy to combat this foe, while obviously aimed at attacking the potential demagogue, concentrated on exploring ways to restore the moral fiber of society through religion and education. Thus, even in defining the greatest political threat to the

86. James H. Smylie, "American Clergymen and the Constitution of the United States of America, 1781–1796" (Ph.D. diss., Princeton Theological Seminary, 1958), pp. 167–168, 176–77, 185.

87. Cumings, *A Sermon Preached before His Honor Thomas Cushing*, pp. 44, 18; Tappan, *The Question Answered*, p.15.

88. Cumings, *A Sermon Preached before His Honor Thomas Cushing*, p. 18; Turner, *Due Glory to be Given to God*, p. 33.

republic, the clergy could not avoid bending politics in an ethical direction.

In thus predicting the republic's moral and political vulnerability—the weakest line of defense and the most formidable opponent—the clergy defined channels of thinking which would direct their own response to the rise of the Democratic Republicans. In the fall of 1794 President Washington denounced before both Houses of Congress certain "self-created societies" which in the context of the Whiskey Rebellion had "assumed a tone of condemnation" of his administration.[89] Like the growing number of partisan Federalists, Congregational ministers picked up the theme and categorically denounced Democratic clubs as representing the kind of sedition that a Republic could not withstand. In expressing his fear of the spirit of faction engendered by these societies, David Osgood traced the source of the problem to "men of ambition, who covet the chief seats in government, [and] exert all their abilities to ingratiate themselves with the source of power." In a monarchy, of course, these men would serve as the flattering courtiers of the king, but in a republic "the same men appear in the character of flaming patriots, profess the warmest zeal for liberty, and call themselves the *friends* of the people." In the finest traditions of republicanism, Osgood condemned the democratic clubs because their artful leaders controlled the members as "mere tools and dupes." "The moment a man is attached to a club, his mind is not free."[90] Attributing to the aspiring democratic leaders the same base

89. Vernon Stauffer, *New England and the Bavarian Illuminati*, p. 109.
90. David Osgood, *The Wonderful Works of God* . . . (Boston, 1794), pp. 22, 26. This bombast provoked great controversy and ran through six pamphlet editions. One Federalist newspaper remarked that Osgood knew "by the roar of the Jacobins," that he "had bitten them in a sore place." See Shipton, *Sibley's Harvard Graduates*, 27: 570–80.

motives once assigned to the tyrants of Britain, the Federalist clergy saw their earlier predictions about democratic tyranny fulfilled before their eyes. How could they escape the conclusion that "these irregular and unwarrantable associations ought to be guarded against and suppressed with a vigilance like that with which we extinguish a fire when it is kindling in a great city"?[91]

The intensification of partisan politics in the last five years of the century only made the devious motives of anti-Federalists seem more pronounced to the pulpit. Since the object of ambitious men in a republic was too diffuse "to flatter or to bribe," they had to "address the more popular passions, and play on strings that particular circumstances, or events, have attuned to their purpose, or that vibrate more in unison with the public pulse." With virtue everywhere on the decline, the clergy fully expected the populace "to mistake party spirit for patriotism, and partisans for men of principle."[92]

This tradition was amply displayed when Nathanael Emmons, the respected minister of Wrentham, Massachusetts, in 1801 devoted a fast sermon to the "strange and deplorable event" which brought the base and ambitious King Jeroboam to the throne of Israel. Without ever naming Thomas Jefferson, Emmons described in unmistakable terms the newly elected American president and condemned the wicked spirit that "led him to prostitute his fine abilities to the vilest purpose." In contrast to his two immediate predecessors, David and Solomon, both wise and illustrious princes, Jeroboam persuaded "the unthinking multitudes, that they were unreasonably loaded with taxes, and that they ought to

91. Osgood, *The Wonderful Works of God*, p. 26.
92. Joseph Buckminster, *The Duty of Republican Citizens* ... (Portsmouth, N. H., 1796), pp. 14, 13.

do themselves justice, by overturning the government."
His techniques were to employ secretly "every artifice to
prejudice the people against the former administration
... and he caused this disaffection, by basely misrepre-
senting the wise measures of that wise and excellent
ruler." In attributing this devastating coup to both
"artful and designing politicians" and to "POLITICAL
DELUSIONS," Emmons not only saw the ultimate
realization of the fearsome political expectations of the
Critical Period, but he also identified as the source of this
political calamity the same problem of moral pollution:
"These great and prevailing delusions ... are not innocent errors, but national iniquities. They display the depravity of the heart rather than the weakness of the
understanding."[93]

ॐ

The Critical Period, far from representing a barren intellectual wasteland between the excited responses of New
England to the American and the French Revolutions,
suggests both the form and content of a fascinating ex-

---

93. Nathanael Emmons, *A Discourse Delivered on the Annual Fast
...* (Wrentham, Conn., 1801), pp. 3, 5, 6, 10, 12, 13, 24, 33–34. According
to Linda K. Kerber, "Federalists insisted that they would have retained their
office had the American people not been deceived. The fault lay not with
republican government, but with the capacity of the opposition for deceptive
techniques, and with the understandable human propensity to listen to those
who spoke of happiness rather than of stern duty or of rectitude." See Kerber,
Federalists in Dissent: Imagery and Ideology in Jeffersonian America (Ithaca,
N. Y., 1970), p. 207. A refreshing exception to the chorus of denunciations of
Jefferson comes from the respected old New Hampshire minister Samuel
Macclintock. As a young man he had battled the French; in the prime of life, the
British; and in the early years of the republic had remained an accepted member
of the Standing Order. By 1800, however, as he approached the venerable age
of three score and ten, his unbending commitment to religious liberty led him to
warmly endorse Jefferson as the future hope of the nation. Shipton, *Sibley's
Harvard Graduates,* 13 (Boston, 1965), 102–12.

cursion. Historians have easily dismissed the tale of a band whose political pilgrimage eventually led them to oppose what most Americans have come to hold dear. The clergy's cause seemed enlightened and progressive when resisting Britain, but in opposing Jefferson and the coming of democracy, it has been viewed as a self-serving rejection of the spirit of seventy-six or, worse yet, irrational and paranoid. While it is certainly easier to identify with clergymen when they were Revolutionaries rather than Federalists, it is equally important to understand how men at the turn of the century could sincerely believe that they were the authentic defenders of liberty's sacred cause. John Lathrop, for instance, active in politics throughout the last twenty-five years of the century, called himself a patriot of seventy-five when he accused the "patriots of 98 and 99" of serving the purposes of foreign nations.[94] Congregationalists argued that theirs was a pure strain of Christian republicanism, well-reasoned, self-consistent. While not taking them half as seriously as they took themselves, the historian must be impressed with those contours of New England thought that did remain stable over time. Even when Yankee clergymen seemed to have broken completely with past reality, concocting the Bavarian Illuminati scare, their reasoning comes as no surprise.

On the morning of May 9, 1798, Reverend Jedidiah Morse unveiled to the New North Church in Boston a shocking plot. Supposedly he had documents in his possession to prove that a secret association of anarchists had successfully plotted the French Revolution, and now, from a French power base, was extending its operations to America. His warning that secret agents were at that moment kindling the fires of social revolution spread

94. John Lathrop, *Patriotism and Religion* . . . (Boston, 1799), pp. 15–17.

through Boston and out across New England.[95] Several
weeks later, an agitated David Tappan, professor of
divinity at Harvard, lectured the senior class on the seriousness of this plot.[96] Equally panicked was Yale's President Timothy Dwight. Putting aside the luxury of
buoyant patriotism, he took the occasion of July 4, 1798,
to warn the city of New Haven that the tumult of the end
times was upon them in the form of spies, saboteurs, and
infidels.[97] By fall, the New England pulpit and press were
humming with tales of the Bavarian Illuminati, despite
the feebleness of Jedidiah Morse's attempts to come forward with hard evidence.[98] What values and attitudes led
Yankees to be so receptive to the tales that Jedediah
Morse was spinning?

To the Federalist mind the plot by the Bavarian Illuminati was generated by the same two-pronged attack
against liberty—civil and religious—which had been responsible for the simultaneous schemes of the Quebec
Act and the tax on tea. Hardly more exaggerated in its
paranoia than perceptions of King George as Antichrist,
reactions to this later advance against liberty became the
ultimate plot of those cosmic forces, which having failed
to tip the balance of liberty in favor of despotic tyranny,

95. Jedidiah Morse, *A Sermon Delivered at the New North Church in
Boston* . . . (Boston, 1798).
96. David Tappan, *A Discourse Delivered in the Chapel of Harvard College* . . . (Boston, 1798).
97. Timothy Dwight, *The Duty of Americans at the Present
Crisis* . . . (New Haven, 1798). At least two other Connecticut audiences heard
of the Illuminati conspiracy on July fourth, one in an oration by Timothy
Dwight's brother. See Theodore Dwight, *An Oration Spoken at Hartford* . . . (Hartford, 1798); and John C. Smith, *An Oration Pronounced at
Sharon* . . . (Litchfield, Conn., [1798]).
98. Vernon Stauffer describes the storm of controversy over Morse's revelations in *New England and the Bavarian Illuminati* (New York, 1918). Henry
May points out that a number of influential Presbyterians such as Ashbel
Green, David Ramsay, and Charles Nisbet also found believable the revelations of Morse. See *The Enlightenment in America* (New York, 1976), pp.
268–71.

returned in different form to unseat that fair maiden with a plan "to root out and abolish Christianity, and overturn all civil government."[99] Jeremy Belknap could not help but indict Paris as a coconspirator with London in the ultimate design to eradicate liberty:

> It is curious and amusing, as well as instructive, to observe, how nearly the conduct of France toward us, in the present controversy, resembles that of Britain in a former controversy. . . . the government of Britain once maintained a swarm of crown officers with pensions and places. . . . Just so the French government is boasting of the influence which they have in this country, and of their power to . . . effect a revolution in their own favor.[100]

If the left-wing attack against that building of "civil and religious liberty in the United States" appeared more devious than the earlier right-wing offensive, it was simply because anarchy was always the surest route to tyranny.[101] So devious had "the arm of proud despotism" become that the liberty of France actually represented a "counterfeit millennium": "It is the millennium of Hell! so it is! it is the attempt of Satan to mount the millennial saddle thro' the instrumentality of the Directory."[102]

It made perfectly good sense to New England Federalists that they were the authentic bearers of the torch of republican liberty. If the deluded men in Jefferson's camp continued to parade their opposition to the slightest hint of authoritarian tyranny, they did so because in their simplicity they had underestimated the deceptive power of Antichrist to appear as an Angel of Light—and of liberty. Even according to their own terms, how could Democratic Republicans miss the lessons of ancient history, which revealed that the Greek and

99. Morse, *A Sermon Delivered at the New North Church*, p. 21.
100. Belknap, *A Sermon Delivered on the 9th of May, 1798*, pp. 20, 21.
101. David Austin, *The Millennial Door Thrown Open* . . . (East-Windsor, Conn.), p. 35.
102. Ibid., pp. 25, 27.

Roman republics fell not by the corruption of power but by the delusion of a corrupt people by those who sought power? Why could not all reasonable republicans perceive that which was so clear for New England eyes: "that of those men who have overturned the liberty of republicks, the greatest number have begun their career, by paying obsequious court to the people, commencing demagogues, and ending tyrants"?[103]

As dark and fearsome as prospects appeared, the clergy did not shrink from the answer which emerged to explain the cause of this deception. The European states, representing the Old Roman Empire (and Daniel's fourth beast), had long deceived the world with civil and religious tyranny and the late "universal tyrannical domination" of French infidelity represented "the last stage of antichristian apostasy." This "dying breath" of Daniel's beast terrified Nathan Strong, the influential minister of Hartford's First Church, and provoked him to impassioned rhetoric that his congregation probably had not witnessed since he joined the Connecticut militia in 1776 shortly after his ordination. In 1798, this seasoned veteran of theological and political turmoil envisioned demonic plagues consuming Europe and threatening all who would not "withdraw their embraces." The prospect of American republicans flirting with liberty, equality, and fraternity left this minister panic-stricken before the alarming words: "Come out of her, my people, that ye be not partakers of her sins, and that ye receive not her plagues."[104] A year later the entire Congregational clergy

103. Samuel Parker, A Sermon before His Honor the Lieutenant-Governor . . . (Boston, 1793), p. 36; see also Samuel Williams, A Discourse Delivered before His Excellency Thomas Chittenden . . . (Rutland, Vt., 1794), p. 23.
104. Nathan Strong, Political Instruction from the Prophecies of God's Word . . . (Hartford, 1798), pp. 11, 9, 14, 5. For an almost identical apocalyptic interpretation of French infidelity, see Timothy Dwight, The Duty of Americans at the Present Crisis . . . (New Haven, 1798).

of Massachusetts, assembled in annual convention, formulated and published an address that applied the same text to the crisis at hand: "Come out of the infidel, antichristian world, my people; that ye be not partakers of her sins, and that ye receive not of her plagues."[105] Conscious that many of their own countrymen had "either embraced or appear approximating towards this infidelity," Yankee ministers could hardly be expected to take democratic arguments seriously.[106] The deception of British tyranny had long since steeled them against bending to the flattery of those whose action aligned them against liberty, both civil and religious.

In confronting their own and the French Revolution, Congregational ministers had defended liberty in the same cosmic framework. In both cases their own *sitz-im-leben* had become the stage for the convulsive struggle of the end times, and the resulting drama found the hosts of good and evil played by a cast who spoke the language of liberty and tyranny. This hybrid of republican and millennial language was surprisingly mature before either revolution. Civil millennialism became a coherent body of thought capable of explaining the threat of despotic tyranny at least fifteen years before the American Revolu-

105. This address is found in the *Independent Chronicle* of July 4, 1799, and the *Newburyport Herald* of June 28, 1799.
106. Strong, *Political Instruction from the Prophecies of God's Word*, p. 27. Several historians have recently described the appalling lack of real communication between opposing factions in the 1790s, among them John R. Howe, Jr.: "By the middle of the decade, American political life had reached the point where no genuine debate, no real dialogue was possible for there no longer existed the toleration of differences which debate requires. Instead there had developed an emotional and psychological climate in which stereotypes stood in the place of reality. In the eyes of Jeffersonians, Federalists became monarchists or aristocrats bent upon destroying America's republican experiment. And Jeffersonians became in Federalist minds social levelers and anarchists, proponents of mob rule." See Howe, "Republican Thought and the Political Violence of the 1790's," *American Quarterly* 19 (1967): 147–65, quotation on p. 150; and Marshall Smelser, "The Federalist Period as an Age of Passion," *American Quarterly* 10 (1958): 391–419.

tion; and the fear of left-wing tyranny prompted by the Critical Period likewise conditioned men and women to define in a certain way problems that they would face in the years after the fall of the Bastille. In both cases it is crucial to understand the ideological filter through which clergymen viewed political change.

Their activities in the Critical Period also point to the root of the clergy's intent to keep the weapons of the new republic cocked in the defense of authority. Unable to believe that any class of men, even the unrestrained tiller of the soil, could act out his virtuous part in the political arena, Yankees scoffed at those who shared the cheerful Jeffersonian assumption that "the foundations of a healthy republic were already present in American society and could be counted on to persist."[107] They demanded a more profound virtue than many other republicans because they believed that selfishness existed in saint and citizen alike and was no mild disease of the soul.

Although this traditional Christian assumption about human nature was strongest in New England's theological heritage, there is little evidence to make a direct correlation between rock-ribbed Calvinism and Federalism or between a milder Arminianism and less concern for order and authority in government. During the 1780s and 1790s severe indictments of the republic were voiced by all manner of Congregational clergymen, Arminian and New Divinity, urban and rural, Harvard- and Yale-trained.[108] The fate of Reverend Ebenezer Bradford, who

107. Kerber, *Federalists in Dissent: Imagery and Ideology in Jeffersonian America*, p. 202.

108. The reactionary political feelings of theological conservatives such as Jedidiah Morse, Timothy Dwight, and Nathanael Emmons may have been expressed with more awesome foreboding, but the substance of their ideas was hardly more right-wing than that of such ministers as Samuel West, Samuel Langdon, Jeremy Belknap, and David Tappan, who were moderate-to-liberal in their theology. James M. Banner has concluded that by 1815 the liberal ministers of Boston had in fact relinquished their tight grip on reactionary

happened to speak in favor of the democratic societies in 1794, reveals that the currents of moral and political feeling ran much deeper than theological distinctions. Nicknamed the "Vandal of Rowley," Bradford was denied other pulpits in his home county of Essex and although not formally expelled by the ministerial association was, in the words of a colleague, "so roughly dealt with that he has not attended its meeting this long time."[109] Political elites in New England continued to offer a negative assessment of human moral character long after a milder theology allowed a more positive judgment. The theologically liberal John Adams, for instance, was as pessimistic when he spoke of politics as the most ardent Edwardsian. Writing to Thomas Jefferson in 1787, Adams made plain his bias:

> I have long been settled in my own opinion that neither Philosophy, nor religion, nor Morality nor Interest, will ever govern nations or Parties, against their Vanity, their Pride, their Resentment or Revenge, or the Avarice or Ambition. Nothing but Force and Power and Strength can restrain them.[110]

How, then, is the particular New England dialect of republicanism to be explained? What intellectual components structured its distinctive explanation of virtue?

---

politics, but it is clear that this later generation of ministers no longer faced convulsive issues like those of the 1790s, having lived to see that a Republican administration did not precipitate social chaos, religious depression, and foreign domination. See Banner, *To the Hartford Convention,* pp. 201–02. It is difficult to understand how Alan Heimert could study New England sermons of this time and argue seriously that Jeffersonian political leanings could be traced to evangelical theology. He misses the mark by 90, if not by 180 degrees, as James W. Davidson has noted in "Searching for the Millennium: Problems for the 1790's and the 1970's," *The New England Quarterly* 45 (1972): 241–61. See Alan Heimert, *Religion and the American Mind: From the Great Awakening to the Revolution* (Cambridge, Mass., 1966), pp. 510–52.

109. Morse, *The Federalist Party in Massachusetts to the Year 1800,* p. 134.

110. Adams to Thomas Jefferson, October 9, 1787, Lester J. Cappon, ed., *The Adams-Jefferson Letters,* 1 (Chapel Hill, N. C., 1959), 202–03.

In general terms, the most satisfying answer to these questions can be found by referring to the ease with which the eighteenth-century Commonwealth tradition merged with New England prophetic history. As the rhetoric of the jeremiad and the coming kingdom slipped so imperceptibly into evocations of republican meanings, it was never divested of certain decidedly reactionary assumptions about the nature of man, society, and government. Thus, throughout the eighteenth century, while political goals increasingly captured the mind of the Yankee minister, the means he turned to continued to issue from a conception of society as fundamentally a moral entity. While the advance of the millennium, for example, became attached to the rise of liberty, the preservation of freedom was linked just as strongly to the increase of Christian virtue. With liberty defined largely in the contemporary terms of civic humanism, virtue retained for many New Englanders connotations as anachronistic as those of Cotton Mather.

This "inside-out" view of republicanism can by no means be taken as the only, or even the primary, force which drove New Englanders toward Federalism. It would be foolish to assume that clergymen spoke definitively for all Federalist leaders; or to deny that a particular social context sent Yankee political elites, lay and clerical alike, scrambling to explain their social position in moral terms. But if one does accept James M. Banner's conclusion that "What drew . . . [men] to Federalism was a mental association with established authority and an affinity for the fixed and traditional,"[111] it is also impossible to dismiss the impact of this reactionary definition of virtue, lodged so close to the heart of New England republican conviction. The skepticism with

111. Banner, *To the Hartford Convention*, p. 168.

which ministers and other Federalists alike viewed the moral capacity of man as citizen stands as the cornerstone of a religious structure embodying a corporate view of society, a positive definition of authority, an alarm at non-Christian as well as individualistic behavior, and the perpetual dread that anarchy was the surest road to tyranny. That these reactionary social and political expectations were sustained and energized by the force of biblical rhetoric points to the need for religious historians to tackle the subject of New England Federalism even though it is a less "usable" history than, say, the New England clergy during the American Revolution. When studied in such light, moreover, the Federalist persuasion and its demand for a republic of Christian virtue stand in striking contrast to the adaptive role of New England religion in the American Revolutionary crisis and may well demonstrate the most direct impact of religion upon politics in eighteenth-century America.

Chapter Four

Visions of a Republican Millennium:
An Ideology of Civil Religion in the New Nation

And may we not view it, at least, as probable, that the expansion of
republican forms of government will accompany that spreading of
the gospel, in its power and purity, which the scripture prophecies
represent as constituting the glory of the latter days?
                                                    John Mellen, 1797

The Second Great Awakening, like its namesake a generation removed, was driven by the compelling hope of
clergymen that their labors would be instrumental in establishing the kingdom of God on earth. Unlike the sudden ebb
of revivalism in the 1740s, however, this later wave of
religious fervor sustained its momentum throughout the
first half of the nineteenth century and swelled the tide of
millennial anticipation throughout Protestant America.
With reference to the many prophetic signs heralding the
kingdom, Lyman Beecher captured the spirit characteristic
of his age:

Soon will the responsive song be heard from every nation, and kindred,
and tongue and people, as the voice of a great multitude, and as the voice
of many waters, and as the voice of mighty thunderings, saying,
Alleluia, for the Lord God Omnipotent reigneth.[1]

Contemporary historians have been fascinated with this
theme as a way of understanding the pervasive identification of the destiny of the American republic with the course
of redemptive history.[2] Not only had the brightness of the

1. Lyman Beecher, *A Reformation of Morals Practicable and Indispensable*
(Andover, Mass., 1814), p. 30.
2. Several historians interested in the religious dimensions of American
culture have recently found a major organizing principle in the convergence of
millennialism and American nationalism. See Ernest L. Tuveson, *Redeemer*

new morning made clear the imminence of the kingdom; it had also suggested that America was to be "both the locus and instrument of the great consummation."[3] This millennial persuasion, buoyant with the civil and religious ideals of the young republic, functioned as a primary idiom of that distinct form of evangelical civic piety that historians have called a "religion of the Republic" or an American civil religion.[4] Whatever the exact contours of this tendency to attribute to the nation "purposive functions, universal and catholic in scope,"[5] historians have generally agreed that Protestantism in the Age of Jackson aligned national purpose so closely with religious conviction that gradually, in the words of John E. Smylie, "the nation emerged as the primary agent of God's meaningful activity in history."[6]

Nation: The Idea of America's Millennial Role (Chicago, 1968); Martin E. Marty, Righteous Empire: The Protestant Experience in America (New York, 1970); and Robert T. Handy, A Christian America: Protestant Hopes and Historical Realities (New York, 1971). This emphasis stands in the tradition of two earlier classics, Ralph Henry Gabriel, The Course of American Democratic Thought (New York, 1940) and H. Richard Niebuhr, The Kingdom of God in America (New York, 1935); and also plays a considerable part in the analyses of Perry Miller, The Life of the Mind in America (New York, 1965), pp. 49–72; Timothy L. Smith, Revivalism and Social Reform: American Protestantism on the Eve of the Civil War (New York, 1965), pp. 225–37; and Ernest Sandeen, The Roots of Fundamentalism: British and American Millenarianism, 1800–1930 (Chicago, 1970).

    3. James F. Maclear, "The Republic and the Millennium," in The Religion of the Republic, ed. Elwyn A. Smith (Philadelphia, 1971), p. 200.

    4. Elwyn A. Smith, ed., The Religion of the Republic. See also Sidney Mead, "The 'Nation with the Soul of a Church.' " Church History 36 (1967): 262–83. Since Robert M. Bellah published the influential article "Civil Religion in America," Daedalus 96 (1967): 1–21, there has been a lively scholarly debate whether or not it is valid to speak of a civil religion in contemporary America. During much of the nineteenth century, however, evangelical Protestantism was the dominant ideology of the nation, an overarching pattern of beliefs to which scholars generally apply the term. See Russell E. Richey and Donald G. Jones, American Civil Religion (New York, 1974) and Henry Warner Bowden, "A Historian's Response to the Concept of American Civil Religion," Journal of Church and State 17 (1975): 495–505.

    5. John E. Smylie, "National Ethos and the Church," Theology Today 20 (1963): 315.

    6. Smylie, "National Ethos and the Church," p. 314. Sidney Mead develops this theme extensively in "The 'Nation with the Soul of a Church,' " Church History 36 (1967): 262–83; see also the works cited in note 2.

It has been an intriguing but complicated task to explain how the kingdom of God and the virtuous republic became for Americans one and the same empire. While students have concurred that visions of a Christian America inspired and motivated American reformers, benevolent volunteers, and foreign missionaries, they have explained the genesis of civil religion in a variety of ways, three of which deserve attention. Some scholars have linked the nineteenth-century ideal of a Christian America to the unsettling pluralism of competing denominations. Others have found a plausible explanation in American fears that waves of social instability and religious confusion would engulf the young nation as they had the French republic. A third perspective has taken note of the ease with which American churches accommodated their message to an age of romantic nationalism. Either alone or in combination, these explanations have provided the most satisfying answers recently given to the question of how the idea of the millennial kingdom became so profoundly Americanized by the second quarter-century of national experience.

The most widely accepted of these attempts to unearth the foundations of civil religion has found them resting upon the bedrock of American denominationalism. According to Sidney Mead, the establishment of religious freedom in America did not undermine the ancient assumption that the well-being of society depended upon commonly shared religious beliefs. The resulting tension forced America's Protestant communions to relax their exclusive claims to truth and pressured them to admit that some "brooding higher unity" lay at the core of all their teachings.[7] In such a context, where multiple religious institutions cancelled out each other's exclusive claims, Americans began to grope for a communal identity to which they could assign an ultimate and inclusive function. That institution

7. Mead, "The 'Nation with the Soul of a Church,' " p. 273.

was, or became, the nation. The emergence of denominationalism thus transformed traditional understand-
ings of the church; the concept of a chosen nation replaced
that of an ecclesiastical community of the redeemed. The
nation developed "the soul of a church" because no American denomination could any longer make such a claim.[8]

If the mosaic composition of American Protestantism
has offered some scholars an explanation of how the
republic was seen as a redemptive instrument, others
have suggested that the vision of a Christian America
expressed the anxieties of troubled ministers "asserting
the unity of culture in pressing danger of fragmenta-
tion."[9] In his highly influential article, "From the Covenant to the Revival," Perry Miller argued that although
the new religious nationalism of the Second Great Awakening developed in some measure as a reaction to disestablishment, its more important source was the intense
desire to preserve the Union from the centrifugal forces of
skeptical rationalism and social anarchy. Confronted
with disruptive internal confusion as well as the ideology
of the French Revolution, a "volcano" which
"threatened to sweep the United States into its fiery
stream,"[10] ministers sought an alternate program for

8. Ibid., p. 262. See also Sideny Mead, *The Lively Experiment: The Shaping of Christianity in America* (New York, 1963), pp. 62–66. By a somewhat different route, James F. Maclear likewise finds disestablishment to be the crucial factor in bringing about the civic faith of the new republic. He argues with respect to New England that the Puritan theocratic tradition emerged with new vitality between 1800 and 1820 because the pressure of religious pluralism forced ministers of the Standing Order to construct a more inclusive ideal of Christian society. See Maclear, " 'The True American Union' of Church and State: The Reconstruction of the Theocratic Tradition," *Church History* 28 (1959): 41–62. Jerald C. Brauer attributes a similar catalytic function to disestablishment in "The Rule of the Saints in American Politics," *Church History* 27 (1958): 240–55.

9. Perry Miller, "From the Covenant to the Revival," in *The Shaping of American Religion,* ed. J. W. Smith and A. L. Jamison (Princeton, N.J., 1961), p. 354.

10. Miller, "from the Covenant to the Revival," p. 351.

Christian solidarity. They found it in the revival and proclaimed its message in the form of a new romantic patriotism.[11]

While these first two explanations of the origins of civil religion describe it as an attempt to reclaim certain cherished values of the past in the face of an unnerving present, the third locates its source in the surprising degree to which Protestantism was swept along by the reigning climate of opinion. The kingdom of God and the nation became virtually equated, according to this interpretation, because of the readiness of Protestants to adapt their message to the spirit of the age. In contrast to earlier days, when clergymen did not retreat from challenging social assumptions that were alien to their purposes, churchmen after 1800 fell into step with the prevailing attitudes of romantic optimism and national idealism. In outlining "the American Democratic Faith" over three decades ago, Ralph Henry Gabriel emphasized that most Protestants gave a hearty assent to the national credo despite its buoyant secular optimism.[12] Other more recent students of this period have likewise seen civil religion as primarily an accommodation of religion to "the prevailing republican enthusiasm and the cult of progress." In an age of followers, they have argued, Americans produced no prophets to decry their pilgrimage en masse to the altar of romantic nationalism.[13]

Although these three explanations of American civil religion on the surface show little similarity, their differ-

11. Miller, *The Life of the Mind in America*, p. 71. This argument is implicit throughout Charles I. Foster's *The Errand of Mercy: The Evangelical United Front, 1790–1837* (Chapel Hill, N.C., 1960).

12. Ralph Henry Gabriel, *The Course of American Democratic Thought* (New York, 1940), pp. 36–37.

13. Maclear, "The Republic and the Millennium," p. 196; George M. Marsden, *The Evangelical Mind and the New School Presbyterian Experience* (New Haven, Conn., 1970), p. 239; John R. Bodo, *The Protestant Clergy and Public Issues, 1812–1848* (Princeton, N.J., 1954), p. 251.

ent melodies seem to be only improvisations of several themes common to them all. In the first place, they have viewed the substitution of nation for church as an unwanted or unnoticed result of expediency. Far from being the product of consistent reasoning, this substitution seemed to rationalize some other more pressing end— such as the creation of national solidarity—or to locate the point where churchmen adrift upon a democratic sea happened to strike land. Secondly, scholars have assumed that the "religion of the Republic" which emerged during the opening decades of the nineteenth century was a substantial departure from previous configurations of political religion. The same elements which resulted in the Second Great Awakening and the subsequent "Benevolent Empire" served as a catalyst which fused liberty and Christianity, the republic and the kingdom, in the minds of men like Lyman Beecher and Francis Wayland.[14] Enforcing the idea that this civic piety was a phenomenon unique to the age of democratic evangelicalism is a third assumption that in the Federalist era New England orthodoxy and republicanism were mutually exclusive and antagonistic forms of thought. Many scholars have assumed that while clergymen of the 1790s dreamed of society's theocratic destiny, their hopes were the very antithesis of the republican ideas held by French Jacobins abroad and Democratic Republicans at home. In contrast to the evident wedding of biblical and republican themes which historians discern in Jacksonian

14. Elwyn A. Smith argues that the "republican theocrat," a figure embodying both orthodox theism and republican thought, emerged only in the third decade of the nineteenth century. See Smith, "The Voluntary Establishment of Religion," in *The Religion of the Republic,* pp. 168–69. In describing a wedding of New England millennial ideas and republican principles as early as the 1760s, an "apocalyptic whiggism," Ernest L. Tuveson offers a welcome exception to those who discuss civil religion as though it were a product of conditions unique to the nineteenth century. See Tuveson, *Redeemer Nation: The Idea of America's Millennial Role,* pp. 20–25.

America, they have pictured New England Christianity in the 1790s as locked in mortal combat with republican thought.[15]

The focus of these assumptions, sharpened by a scholarly convention that separates the "Middle Period" from the era of the Revolution, has allowed discussion of the "religion of the Republic" to proceed with little reference to the interaction of Christian and republican themes during the last quarter of the eighteenth century. Among other things, the Second Great Awakening has become a starting point to understand the religious patriotism of nineteenth-century America. By contrast, this study gropes forward toward the Great Revival and finds in its New England phase, at least, a fitting culmination of an intellectual tradition shaped during the founding of the republic. Yankee ministers who watched the dawn of the new century did not stumble unawares upon the road of civil religion; they actively sought a way of assigning to the American republic a major role in the scheme of providential history because signposts had for two generations indicated to thoughtful clergymen that the highway leading to the kingdom followed definite political as well as religious principles. Their sense of American destiny followed an older tendency to join theological and republican concerns.[16]

15. This clear dichotomy between New England orthodoxy and secular political theories is evident in Perry Miller, "From the Covenant to the Revival," 350; James F. Maclear, " 'The True American Union' of Church and State: The Reconstruction of the Theocratic Tradition," 41–62; and Jerald C. Brauer, "The Rule of the Saints in American Politics," 240–55.

16. For too long political and religious historians of eighteenth-century America have lived like neighbors who are not on speaking terms. The brilliant volumes published almost simultaneously by Bernard Bailyn and Alan Heimert several years ago make us painfully aware of the difficulties which students experience when they turn to examine the politics of religious conviction. William Gribbin clearly recognizes this point in his suggestive article "Republican Religion and the American Churches in the Early National Period," *The Historian* 35 (1972): 61–74.

During the last half of the eighteenth century, the Great War for the Empire, the first two revolutions of modern times, the founding of a new republic, and the estrangement of Federalist New England from Jeffersonian America prompted and gave character to new directions in religious thought. Overriding civic concerns led New England ministers to recast the major strains of their traditional eschatology. By bringing to the heart of redemptive history the republican values of civil and religious liberty, ministers articulated a civic theology that gave a profoundly new religious significance to the function of man as citizen, to the principles governing the civil order, and to the role of nations in bringing on the millennium. While the acid bath of war corroded in great measure the bonds between church and state elsewhere in America, in New England it seemed to etch in bold relief a view of history which identified the aspirations of the church with the rise of republican liberty. This shift was occasioned by the tumult of war and political upheaval but its real historical import stems from the persisting strength of the new ideological alignment long after the winning of independence. Sustaining political values as religious priorities became habitual among ministers of the early republic; they anticipated a republican millennium.

᭞

New England ministers responded to the founding of the American republic with their own brand of dialectic theology. They were the first to admit that the church had taken a serious beating at the hands of the war's impiety and the victory's "infidelity." Gloomy New England prophets perceived a serious religious depression in America, whether or not one in fact occurred. Yet in remarkable contrast to the anxious tones of their jeremiads, ministers had never been more confident of the kingdom's advance. Millennial expectancy during the last two decades of the century rose to unparalleled heights, while the perceived state of the church experienced the opposite effect.[17] This paradox easily could be understood if the clergy's hopes sprang from a conviction that the darkest part of the night immediately preceded the dawn. But such is hardly the case. At the exact moment, rather, that piety seemed at an all-time low, the clergy proclaimed that the advancing kingdom had delivered

the deadly shock to the last section of the Babylonish Image. . . . The stone braves all opposition and advances and strikes with redoubled strength the feet of the mighty image: It trembles, it reels to and fro, and threatens to fall.[18]

With this and other graphic depictions of the disarray and retreat of antichristian forces, clergymen voiced their confidence that the divine armies were at the point of storming the very gates of hell.[19] The question of how churchmen could rejoice in the unprecedented success of the kingdom while their own churches lay devastated by the enemy suggests a reordering of their allegiance from

17. Only a generation earlier, in the 1740s, the millennial expectancy of Jonathan Edwards and other New Lights rose and fell in a pattern that corresponded with the perceived state of vital religion within the churches.

18. David Austin, *The Millennial Door Thrown Open* . . . (East Windsor, Conn., 1799), pp. 20, 22.

19. Scores of Congregational ministers from 1780 to 1800 expressed an intense conviction that the new day of Christ's kingdom was about to dawn, e.g., David Tappan, *A Discourse Delivered at the Third Parish in Newbury* . . . (Salem, 1783); Ezra Stiles, *The United States Elevated to Glory and Honor* (New Haven, Conn., 1783); Joseph Eckley, *A Sermon Preached at the Request of the Ancient and Honorable Artillery Company* . . . (Boston, 1792); John Mellen, *A Sermon Delivered Before His Excellency the Governor* . . . (Boston, 1797); Jeremy Belknap, *A Sermon, Delivered on the 9th of May, 1798* (Boston, 1798); Nathan Strong, *Political Instruction from the Prophecies of God's Word* . . . (Hartford, 1798).

ecclesia to *polis*. It can be fully answered only by clarifying their republican eschatology.

While the political shock waves of the 1790s raised New England anxieties to unparalleled heights, Congregational ministers never complained that the shattering of order had dulled their ability to explain the inner logic of the political world.[20] By the end of the century their explanations of American and European history had become clearly focused upon certain well-defined interpretations of prophetic Scripture. The most common of these came from Daniel chapter two, which describes Nebuchadnezzar's dream of a great and terrible image that crumbled "like the chaff of the summer threshing floors" before the force of a stone hurled against its feet of iron and clay. After destroying the image, this stone, described by the prophet as "cut out of the mountain without hands," developed into a great mountain that filled the whole earth.[21] Numerous interpreters found in this text a fascinating correlation between the stone and the American Revolution; between the feet of iron and clay and the nations of Europe; and between the growing mountain and the American republic. The meanings attributed to these and other apocalyptic images, moreover, reveal the interlocking providential and republican ideologies so characteristic of New England ministers in the age of the American and French Revolutions.

New England churchmen were emphatic in celebrating the American Revolution as the central event in this republican eschatology. In reflecting on the first twenty years of his country's political experiment, John Cushing of Ashburnham, Massachusetts, suggested in 1796 that

20. The heightened tensions of these years are described ably by Marshall Smelser, "The Federalist Period as an Age of Passion," *American Quarterly* 10 (1958): 391–419; and John R. Howe, Jr., "Republican Thought and the Political Violence of the 1790s," *American Quarterly* 19 (1967): 147–65.

21. Daniel 2:35, 2:45.

"the revolution in America, in a political view, will prove to be the stone cut out of the mountain without hands, which will fill the whole earth."[22] In similar fashion the erratic David Austin took for granted that:

the *political stone* which is now giving the deadly shock to the last section of the Babylonish Image . . . was it not the weighty stone which we all helped to lift, during the introduction and progress of that political revolution through which we have just now passed?[23]

Clergymen were equally forthright to explain their reason for viewing the Revolution as a critical "sign of the times." The American victory became theologically significant to these men because it animated the new nation with the principle of liberty, both civil and religious. The Revolution assumed this lofty role, Joseph Eckley said in 1792, because of the general discussion it "introduced on the subject of national politicks," raising hopes that the day would soon come "when mankind universally shall be free."[24] Elias Lee, a Connecticut Baptist, likewise equated the stone of Daniel with the war against Britain because it had raised "the standard of liberty and republicanism" against the pride and power of monarchy.[25] In

22. John Cushing, *A Discourse, Delivered at Ashburnham* . . . (Leominster, Mass., 1796), p. 19.

23. David Austin, *The Millenial Door Thrown Open*, p. 20. David Austin was undoubtedly an eschatological quack who translated his concern for the end times into such bizarre activities as building dwellings in New Haven for Jews who would assemble prior to the restoration of Israel. As is so often the case, however, Austin's extreme views were not antithetical to the climate of opinion in which he lived. His explicitly political eschatology was but a logical, if sometimes absurd, extension of judgments being made by numerous Congregational and Presbyterian clergymen. James W. Davidson discusses Austin's strange career in "Searching for the Millennium: Problems for the 1790s and the 1970s," *New England Quarterly* 95 (1972): 245–49.

24. Joseph Eckley, *A Sermon Preached at the Request of the Ancient and Honorable Artillery Company*, pp. 18, 13.

25. Elias Lee, *The Dissolution of Earthly Monarchies* . . . (Danbury, Conn., 1794), p. 16. Taken at face value, this obscure clergyman's explanation of the end times is superb witness to the power of political turmoil to move

this scheme, the structure of freedom that arose from the ashes of war clearly became "the base of the approaching building of God."[26]

By thus aligning a scheme of providential history with republican thought, this widely shared perspective on the Revolution made the realization of liberal political goals essential to the approach of the kingdom. The prospect of sharing the political ideals of the Revolution with all mankind became, in this climate of opinion, not only the clergy's fondest hope but also a necessary prerequisite for spreading the Christian message. David Austin stated explicitly this recurring inference:

It seems no unnatural conclusion from ancient prophecy, . . . that in order to usher in . . . the *latter-day-glory,* TWO GREAT REVOLU-TIONS are to take place; the *first* outward and political; the *second* inward and spiritual.[27]

The gospel was only compatible with political forms that stood on the sacred ground of liberty.

Charting providential history by the milestones of civil

---

different men independently to similar convictions. In his preface to the above sermon (p. 4), Lee explained in the third person how he came to perceive civil monarchy as "the mystery of iniquity": "He [Lee] never read an author upon this subject in his life. But about twelve months ago as he was musing on the great outcry in the world, with respect to Monarchy and Republicanism . . . he came at length to his conclusion that there was a necessity of a universal revolution or a disappointment of scripture prophecy."

26. David Austin, *The Millenial Door Thrown Open,* p. 35. Even those who refused to attach great eschatological significance to political affairs offer evidence of the popularity of doing so. The Sabbatarian Baptist Henry Clarke complained: "I have heard and seen in books, many prophecies, calculations, and arguments about the Millennium or thousand year reign of Christ upon earth in the latter day glory of the church, as tho' nigh at hand—and to be brought about by some revolution in the political transactions of the nations of the world, and in the present state of things. But how absurd are such notions!" Clarke, *A History of the Sabbatarians or Seventh Day Baptists in America* (Utica, N.Y., 1811), p. 165.

27. David Austin, *The Millennium* . . . (Elizabethtown, N.J., 1794), pp. 393, 394.

and religious liberty was hardly a novelty for clergymen of the Federalist period. The notion of civil millennialism first became prominent during the Anglo-French wars which took place between 1745 and 1760, and received its most popular defense in John Adams's essay *A Dissertation on the Canon and Feudal Law*. During the Revolutionary crisis such ideas became a conventional pattern of understanding in New England, as evidenced by Samuel Sherwood's comments in 1776:

Liberty has been planted here; and the more it is attacked, the more it grows and flourishes. The time is coming and hastening on, when Babylon the great shall fall to rise no more; when all tyrants and oppressors shall be destroyed forever.[28]

America's recovery of its civil and religious rights in the victory over Britain intensified the conviction. By the end of the century a republican eschatology seemed in retrospect to have fired the American Revolution. It remained firmly enshrined in popular thought and offered a model for the coming age:

No sooner had the *twenty years* of our political operation built for us this political temple; than wisdom fell from God in respect to the millennial temple; . . . and whilst European nations behold on these western shores of the Atlantic, the temple of freedom, over which our confederation spreads its wings, they shall see how delightful a picture of the approaching millennial confederation it presents.[29]

Operating within the same moral framework, Yankee clergymen identified the nations of Europe as primary expressions of antichristian darkness. Jeremy Belknap, like many of his colleagues, demanded that America

28. Samuel Sherwood, *The Church's Flight into the Wilderness: An Address on the Times* (New York, 1776), p. 49.
29. Austin, *The Millennial Door Thrown Open*, p. 30.

remain outside the orbit of European influence. "I detest the thought," he declared, "that any rotten toe of Nebuchadnezzar's image . . . should ever exercise dominion over this country."[30] In his mind the nations of Europe had demonstrated beyond question their character as the feet of iron and clay that would crumble before the stone. Antichrist had chosen these nations, led by Britain and France, to become, in the words of Nathan Strong, "the last stage of anti-christian apostacy."[31] Having grown up in an eschatological tradition that identified the forces of evil with the politics of tyranny, these interpreters in the 1790s quite naturally assumed that "in the language of prophecy, tyrannical governments, both civil and ecclesiastical, are represented by fierce and destroying beasts . . ."[32] Just as the kingdom advanced by the rise of civil and religious liberty, so the legions of Satan retreated with the demise of the "machinery of papal, and anti-republican despotism."[33]

Federalist clergymen were persuaded that Satan had shifted his primary base of operations from a false church to the governments of certain despotic nations. With remarkable consistency they reiterated the eschatology which Samuel Sherwood and Samuel West had proclaimed at the outbreak of the American Revolution. "Until of late," wrote David Austin in 1799, Protestant divines had all "united in applying" the image of Antichrist to "the papal power." This had obviously been an

30. Jeremy Belknap, *A Sermon, Delivered on the 9th of May, 1798,* p. 19.
31. Nathan Strong, *Political Instruction from the Prophecies of God's Word,* p. 9. Strong went on to say (p. 20) that "the co-estates of the Old Roman empire, although under different sovereigns, and often at mutual enmity, have formed a body distinct from the rest of mankind, and have stretched the iron hand of their influence to the end of the earth."
32. Ibid., p. 10.
33. Charles Turner, *Due Glory to be Given to God* (Boston, 1783), p. 32.

error, he continued, because the feet of Nebuchadnezzar's image were "formed of *iron and of clay;* of kingly
and of priestly power combined." Against both, he
cried, "the stone is now striking."[34] In a similar vein,
David Osgood analyzed the weakness of the Pope
in the eighteenth century and came to the following
conclusions:

The marks of the beast and of the dragon, so visible and manifest upon
it in ancient times, were nearly obliterated. The mother of harlots had
either become a reformed prostitute, or having passed the days of vig-
our and passion, was a mere withered form in the last stage of de-
crepitude, retaining only the shadow and skeleton of former times.

The power of Satan, instead, had shifted to:

The several systems of tyranny and oppression, of cruelty and persecution, which have preceded the present era [and] are designated in this
book by THE DRAGON, THE BEAST, THE FALSE PROPHET,
BABYLON THE GREAT, THE MOTHER OF HARLOTS, and the
like.[35]

In the perspective of such preachers, Antichrist had taken
up politics as the most devious scheme to thwart Providence and had mounted his attack primarily along national rather than ecclesiastical lines. The Devil, said Elias
Lee is "always busy about civil affairs; and like all other
corrupt politicians endeavoring to turn everything to his
own advantage."[36]

This view of a political Antichrist—the first novel eschatological interpretation of evil since the Reformation
—developed remarkable strength because it could ap-

34. Austin, *The Millennial Door Thrown Open,* pp. 4–6.
35. David Osgood, *The Devil Let Loose . . .* (Boston, 1799), pp. 8, 10.
36. Lee, *The Dissolution of Earthly Monarchies,* p. 11.

propriate for its own purposes the earlier tradition. No less an antichristian symbol than before, the papacy now appeared in alliance with the more awesome legions of civil despotism. "The league or combination, formed between civil and religious monarchies," continued Elias Lee, "is a matter of fact, which none can deny. These are a proper match for each other." They have sometimes quarreled, he admitted, but "like a company of rakes in a tavern; who after a few contradictions and hard blows, drink a bowl, shake hands, and become good friends."[37] History taught the convincing lesson that despotic governments always maintained a religion of the same character.

Yet the turmoil of French politics after the Revolution —what Freeman Parker called a "great apocalyptic earthquake"[38]—convinced clergymen of the same lesson taught by the American Revolution: that tyrannical political power was easily the master of her ecclesiastical counterpart. On the first Sunday of the nineteenth century, Nathan Strong of Hartford assessed the signs of the times in a manner that was becoming commonplace in New England:

The general train of events in the political world, hath been drying up the mystical Euphrates, or diminishing the power and influence of the Antichristian Babylon. Rome has become an insignificant name, and scarcely is a thunder left in her vatican. . . .

Yankees were struck by the "surprising rise of the French empire upon the ruins of papal Europe"[40] and found it a

37. Ibid., pp. 18, 19.
38. Freeman Parker, *A Sermon Delivered at Dresden, July 23, 1812* . . . (Portland, Maine, 1812), p. 8.
39. Nathan Strong, *On the Universal Spread of the Gospel* . . . (Hartford, 1801), p. 36.
40. William Fowler Miller, *A Dissertation on the Harvest of Mystical Babylon* (Hartford, 1808), p. 11.

direct fulfillment of the prophecy of Revelation 17: "The Beast [Napoleonic France] shall hate the Whore [the Roman Church] and shall make her desolate and naked, and shall eat her flesh and burn her with fire."[41] A despotic nation clearly had subdued the ecclesiastical embodiment of evil and reconfirmed for those petrified by French infidelity that the cosmic struggle between good and evil had shifted to national governments and the political principles they embodied. The only proper match for a nation that combined tyrannies in state and church was a nation that defended itself by a union of "civil and religious republicanism, or in other words, civil and religious liberty."[42]

The American republic came for very good reason to seem the primary agent of redemptive history. While a church might espouse Christian freedom, only a nation could preserve the civil liberty which was its prerequisite. The force of this logic seemed even greater when ministers considered the means necessary to initiate the kingdom. The conviction became common that republican liberty was essential not only to the free presentation of the gospel but also to its ready understanding by those who heard it. Gad Hitchcock suggested that while men enjoying liberty could be motivated by religion, those deprived of it "become stupid, and debased in spirit, indolent and groveling, indifferent to all valuable improvement, and hardly capable of any."[43] Even if tyrannical governments began to grant that religious freedom

41. From 1800 until 1812, this interpretation of Revelation 17 became standard for Francophobe Yankees. See Strong, On the Universal Spread of the Gospel, p. 36; Eli Smith, The Signs of the Times . . . (Amherst, N. H., 1804), p. 5; Timothy Dwight, A Discourse in Two Parts, Delivered August 20, 1812 . . . (New York, 1812), p. 12; Thomas Andros, The Grand Era of Ruin to Nations from Foreign Influence (Boston, 1812), pp. 7–8.
42. Lee, The Dissolution of Earthly Monarchies, p. 11.
43. Gad Hitchcock, A Sermon Preached at Plymouth December 22d, 1774 (Boston, 1775), p. 17.

which they had always opposed, servile minds might well continue to shut out the light of truth.

The logical outcome of giving such high priority to civil freedom was to identify the expansion of American republicanism with the growth of Daniel's mountain.[44] John Mellen of Barnstable made the point explicit:

And may we not view it, at least, as probable, that the expansion of republican forms of government will accompany that spreading of the gospel, in its power and purity, which the scripture prophecies represent as constituting the glory of the latter days?[45]

Following the logic of their own eschatology, clergymen placed the American nation at the center of redemptive history. They knew that only a republic could "wake up and encourage the dormant flame of liberty in all quarters of the earth . . . and thereby open and prepare . . . minds for the more easy reception of the truth and grace of the gospel."[46]

༄

This vision of history moving toward a republican millennium was a reflection of a much deeper commitment whereby the gospel became linked inseparably with a libertarian political order. It was hardly a passing phase of high hopes for the new political experiment or the blurred impression of men failing to distinguish between providential and republican images while under the ex-

44. Lee, *The Dissolution of Earthly Monarchies*, p. 16; Belknap, *A Sermon, Delivered on the 9th of May, 1798*, pp. 18–19, 26.

45. John Mellen, *A Sermon Delivered Before his Excellency the Governor*, p. 28.

46. Tappan, *A Discourse Delivered at the Third Parish in Newbury*, p. 12.

citement of apocalypse. At the very heart of New England social consciousness, the ideal Christian commonwealth became indistinguishable from that of a model republic. Men who expected a future kingdom of liberty evidenced a continuing assumption that:

No form of government yet constructed, ever was so congenial to christianity, as a well regulated Republic. No religion, ever yet known, is so conformable to the genius of a free government, as christianity.[47]

The most crucial aspect of this Christian republicanism is its function as an idiom through which intense Christian beliefs and symbols came to focus on the preservation of republican principle. The cause of liberty thus became a sacred one. Ministers read libertarian ideals into the experience of Old Testament Israel, expressed opposition to vice with republican jeremiads, promoted Christian education in order to ensure national well-being, and identified the rise of "infidelity" as part of a political conspiracy. An examination of these four clerical perspectives from 1780 to 1800 will reveal that in each case New England religion prompted its adherents to attribute to the republic "purposive functions, universal and catholic in scope."[48]

During the second half of the eighteenth century Congregational ministers from one end of the theological spectrum to the other came to include political liberty as a fundamental article of faith. A settled and almost unquestioned conviction reigned that "LIBERTY is the spirit and genius, not only of the gospel, but the whole of that

47. Jonathan French, *A Sermon Preached Before His Excellency Samuel Adams* . . . (Boston, 1796), pp. 6–7.
48. Smylie, "National Ethos and the Church," p. 315.

revelation, we have first and last, received from God."[49] Time and again ministers who reflected on the course of salvation history argued that the people of God had always defended civil and religious liberty. They found their own values reflected most clearly in the past when they searched for their own identity in the Old Testament and there found, in the words of a sermon title by Samuel Langdon, *The Republic of the Israelites an Example to the American States*.[50] Reading the Pentateuch in the light of a libertarian theology John Mellen concluded that "even the law and institution of *Moses*, . . . was yet founded in freedom, and was favorable to the cause of liberty."[51]

Earlier eighteenth-century ministers believed that certain variations of monarchy, aristocracy, and democracy were more in keeping with scriptural principle than others, but had always thought it impossible to assign a divine mandate to any particular form. Samuel West, for instance, as late as 1776 said that one could not determine "what particular form of government is best for a community,—whether a pure democracy, aristocracy, monarchy or a mixture of all of these simple forms." They all had advantages and disadvantages.[52] By the end

49. John Mellen, *The Great and Happy Doctrine of Liberty* (Boston, 1795), p. 9. Charles Turner observed that a "*true* spirit of liberty" was "nothing more nor less than a spirit of true Christianity, considered as extending itself in reference to matters of civil and ecclesiastical government." See Turner, *Due Glory to be Given to God*, p. 29; and Levi Hart, *Liberty Described and Recommended* . . . (Hartford, 1775), who argued (p. 8) that "the gospel of our salvation is principally taken up in describing that glorious liberty which is purchased for sinners by the Son of God."

50. Samuel Langdon, *The Republic of the Israelites an Example to the American States* (Exeter, N.H., 1788). See also Abiel Abbot, *Traits of Resemblance in the People of the United States of America to Ancient Israel* (Haverhill, Mass., 1799).

51. Mellen, *The Great and Happy Doctrine of Liberty*, p. 9.

52. Samuel West, *A Sermon Preached before the Honorable Council* . . . (Boston, 1776), p. 22.

of the Revolution, however, and for the remainder of the century, that which ministers had seen through a glass darkly became clearly visible. "The only form of government expressly instituted by heaven was that of the Hebrews," James Dana maintained in 1779. "Theirs was a confederate republic with JEHOVAH at the head."[53] Clergymen in the new nation pictured in great detail the republican spirit and structure of Israel's early government. Its constitution was "most friendly to public liberty. . . . Equality of condition was provided for, and the means of corruption prevented. . . ." In order to preserve their liberties, God had instructed the Israelites to remember their bondage in Egypt and "the manifest interposition of the Almighty in humbling tyrants for their sakes."[54] Joseph Huntington declared that the republic of Israel was a confederacy of "Thirteen United States or tribes," reminding parishioners who remembered only twelve that the tribe of Joseph had been subdivided into Ephraim and Manasseh, "which made thirteen *united, free and independent states.*" The united states of Israel moreover had a "General Congress," and a "president at their head."[55] Ancient Israel thus mirrored to Christian republicans of New England a remarkably clear image of their own developing institutions.

That clergymen found republican ideals confirmed in the experience of Israel is significant for two important reasons. For over a century New England had found her deepest sense of religious identity as the new Israel. The

53. James Dana, *A Sermon Preached Before the General Assembly* . . . (Hartford, 1779), p. 17. The following year, Samuel Cooper's sermon on Massachusetts's new constitution likewise identified the government of the Hebrew nation as a "free republic" established originally "by a charter from Heaven." See Cooper, *A Sermon Preached Before His Excellency John Hancock* . . . (Boston, 1780), p. 8.

54. Dana, *A Sermon Preached Before the General Assembly,* p. 17.

55. Joseph Huntington, *A Discourse Adapted to the Present Day* . . . (Hartford, 1781), pp. 9–10.

hermeneutic which allowed an exact parallel between the two societies translated positive Old Testament events into divine admonitions, and made of covenant-breaking a very serious affair. In picturing God's ancient covenant people as a republic, therefore, ministers gave to the defense of liberty the full force of religious argument. The preservation of the republic, far from posing an idolatrous challenge to the covenant, became fulfillment of the law.

The republican imagery about Israel is also significant as an idiom through which notions of collective religious identity were sustained long after the original Puritan concept of the social covenant had lost its hold. The Revolutionary generation affirmed no less intensely than their forebears that their society had been divinely chosen, but they had expanded the primary terms of obligation to include republican liberty. Their own priorities were reshaped to accord with changes in society at large, though its rhetoric remained Puritan. Having redefined religious priorities in republican terms, New Englanders found their sense of mission less flawed than ever before. While Puritan Boston had never really attracted much outside attention as a city on a hill, republican America offered a beacon of liberty that all could see.

New England ministers in the 1780s and 1790s vacillated between an attitude of hope inspired by the achievements of American liberty and a sense of foreboding occasioned by the spread of national vice. They had every reason to see the United States as a harbinger of the millennium when contrasted with European despotism; but with respect to the demands of a national covenant, they knew that accents of jeremiad were much more appropriate. These jeremiads, however, became no less a quest for republican continuity than either the vision of the coming kingdom or the history of ancient Israel. Just as that which bolstered the clergy's confidence was America's position as the asylum of republican principle, so that which aroused apprehension was fear that the republic would collapse.

The birth of the United States produced in New England a rebirth of the traditional jeremiad. Anxious ministers thundered against the age-old vices of "luxury, dissipation, extravagance, gaming, idleness and intemperance."[56] While the content of these intensified warnings remained virtually unchanged, the interlocking motivation of judgment and promise that gave force to the jeremiad assumed a form decidedly contemporary. What kind of destruction lay at the end of the broad road of vice? What quality of life greeted the few who chose the narrow path of virtue? Levi Frisbie expressed the common answer to these questions with the following warning:

If we sink into carelessness and indolence, pride and luxury, folly and dissipation; if envy, selfishness, avarice and ambition; if any or all of this brood of execrable vices gain a predominant influence over us, they will misguide our councils, corrupt our governments, enervate our strength, destroy our order and security, *dissolve our union*. . . .[57]

Frisbie feared that vice would bring swift and certain ruin to the government of liberty that Americans were struggling to erect. Similarly, Samuel Macclintock described

56. Samuel Macclintock, *A Sermon Preached Before the Honorable Council* . . . (Portsmouth, N.H., 1784), p. 35. Far from removing the strictures of the jeremiad, victory over Britain intensified the clergy's moral anxiety. David Tappan's attitude was quite typical: "If this then has been the state and progress of things, while we have been under the fetters and terrors of war, what are we to expect, now these restraints are taken off, and our unsubdued lusts permitted to range and riot at large among the tempting sweets of a fertile, peaceful country, and to call in to their entertainment the delicacies and luxuries of all foreign climes?" Tappan, *The Question Answered* . . . (Salem, 1783), p. 15.

57. Levi Frisbie, *An Oration, Delivered at Ipswich* . . . (Boston, 1783), p. 22.

the jeremiad's traditional list of vices as "diseases of the political body, which prey upon its very vitals, and by certain, tho' insensible degrees, bring on its dissolution." Other ministers likewise found that their greatest tool of motivation was to depict the end of sin as "Bribery, corruption and tyranny" or "the ruin of republican States."[58] "A NATION favored with gospel privileges," declared William Symmes, "cannot slight and neglect their religious advantages, without endangering their civil liberties."[59] Within the scope of this republican jeremian even the confession of sin seemed an affirmation of the principles of liberty; a Vermont minister went so far as to affirm that love of country might "be improved as a powerful motive to religion."[60]

If the reordering of Israel into a commonwealth of liberty revealed that republican faith pervaded religious commitment, this renewed jeremiad also recast the character of Providence in a republican mold. In defining the consequence of continued vice, ministers clearly stipulated the cyclical pattern of growth and decline that all republics had followed in keeping with their own moral character. "Experience proves that political bodies, like the animal economy, have their periods of infancy, youth, maturity, decay, and dissolution," remarked David Tappan in a fast sermon on the text, "Righteousness exalteth a nation; but sin is a reproach to any people."[61] He viewed the history of the ancient Greek and Roman republics to be highly instructive to the

58. Macclintock, *A Sermon Preached Before the Honorable Council*, p. 35; Dana, *A Sermon Preached Before the General Assembly*, p. 41; Jeremy Belknap, *An Election Sermon Preached Before the General Court of New Hampshire* . . . (Portsmouth, N.H., 1785), p. 27.
59. William Symmes, *A Sermon Preached Before His Honor Thomas Cushing* . . . (Boston, 1785), pp. 20–21.
60. Dan Foster, *An Election Sermon; Delivered Before the Honorable Legislature of the State of Vermont* . . . (Windsor, Vt., 1790), p. 23.
61. David Tappan, *A Discourse, Delivered to the Religious Society in Brattle-Street* . . . (Boston, 1798), pp. 18, 5.

people of America. "The prosperity, declension, and ruin of those states," he said, "show that virtue is the soul of republican freedom."[62] By consistently identifying the fate of fallen republics with the divine judgment inherent in the jeremiad, ministers witnessed the Lord and Judge of history carrying out his purposes through the unchanging laws which governed the political order. Men were called to renounce sin not by the Ancient of Days whose sword of judgment might at any moment rend the veil of time but rather by ties of intense loyalty to that republic to which God had chosen to limit His program of kingdom renewal. The clear note of God's immediacy, once the trumpet call that struck fear into New England hearts, had become only a memory brought to mind by the muffled tones of a distant Providence echoing through the cycles of republican history.[63]

New England had always considered education the appropriate antidote for those diseases of vice diagnosed by the jeremiad. The necessity of perpetuating a Christian commonwealth had for one hundred and fifty years instilled the firm belief that:

Tis education forms the common mind;
Just as the twig is bent the tree's inclin'd.[64]

This same rationale accompanied the post-Revolutionary resurgence of the jeremiad as clergymen voiced repeated

62. Ibid., p. 19.
63. J. G. A. Pocock elaborates the cyclical view of politics by which Americans schooled in the traditions of radical Whiggery saw the growth and decay of republics as a function of the changing civic virtue which each embodied. See "Civic Humanism and its Role in Anglo-American Thought," in Pocock, *Politics, Language and Time: Essays on Political Thought and History* (New York, 1971), pp. 80–103. James M. Banner discusses the convergence of this strain with traditional New England ideas of providential history in *To the Hartford Convention: The Federalists and the Origins of Party Politics in Massachusetts, 1789–1815* (New York, 1970), pp. 32–36.
64. Simeon Doggett, *A Discourse on Education* . . . (New Bedford, Mass., 1796), p. 1.

concern that education should be the first object of civil
and religious authorities.[65] Their observations reveal
from a third perspective the power of republicanism to
color Christian belief.

Like their ancestors, clergymen in the new nation
pointed to education as the primary means for "the improvement of youth, in that christian practical godliness,
public spirit and virtue, which would exclude the vile
oppressing passions from their hearts."[66] But unlike the
early Puritans, ministers in the United States were well
versed in another intellectual tradition that gave education an equally crucial role, a conviction that "ignorance
and liberty are incompatible"[67] and that "in a republican
government the whole force of education is required."[68]
That the rhetoric of New England clergymen had har-
nessed the energy of both traditions is hardly an unexpected conclusion given the preceding discussion. Their
views on education demonstrate not only that their
ideology became a Christian republicanism but, furthermore, that this concern for "Christian and republican
education" in certain ways subordinated the former to
the latter.

As early as 1765 John Adams had argued for the

65. New England ministers devote as much rhetoric to the necessity of
proper education as they do to any other single theme, e.g., Samuel Stillman,
An Oration, Delivered July 4th, 1789... (Boston, 1789), p. 25; Belknap, *An
Election Sermon Preached Before the General Court of New Hampshire*, pp.
18–19; Samuel Williams, *A Discourse Delivered Before His Excellency
Thomas Chittenden*... (Rutland, Vt., 1794), p. 25; Caleb Blood, *A Sermon
Preached Before the Honorable Legislature*... (Rutland, Vt., 1792), p. 28;
Samuel Macclintock, *A Sermon Preached Before the Honorable Council*, p.
37. Gordon S. Wood points to the heightened concern for education which
gripped many Americans determined to preserve republican institutions. See
The Creation of the American Republic, 1776–1787, pp. 120, 426.
66. Turner, *Due Glory to be Given to God*, p. 29.
67. Samuel Parker, *A Sermon, Preached Before His Honor the
Lieutenant-Governor*... (Boston, 1793), p. 41.
68. Dana, *A Sermon Preached Before the General Assembly*, p. 39.

importance of education by combining the traditional New England rationale with the Whig understanding that education was the prerequisite of political liberty. In idealizing the opposition of his forefathers to tyranny in church and state, Adams defended education's twofold purpose:

Their civil and religious principles, therefore, conspired to prompt them to use every measure and take every precaution in their power to propagate and perpetuate knowledge.[69]

Ignorance was for Adams the bane of European history because, under the guise of Christianity, the union of ecclesiastical and civil tyranny had reduced the mind of men "to a state of sordid ignorance."[70] As long as this confederacy between the canon and feudal laws continued, it held men in ignorance; and it suppressed liberty and virtue through one age of darkness after another. Only since the time of the Reformation had men been able to seek and to find knowledge so crucial to the life of freedom in government and religion.[71]

The drive for education among New England churchmen followed explicitly this line of thought. "Despotic governments," said Joseph Eckley, " . . . always maintain their strength proportionate to the degree of ignorance among the people."[72] Christian republicans found this kind of ignorance so terrifying because it was a tool of miter and scepter. Despotic forces in church and state had suppressed education, knowing well that "an ignorant people will easily receive idolatry for their religion,

69. John Adams, *A Dissertation on the Canon and Feudal Law*, in *The Works of John Adams*, ed. Charles Francis Adams, 3 (Boston, 1851), 455.
70. Ibid., p. 450.
71. Ibid., pp. 448–56.
72. Eckley, *A Sermon Preached at the Request*, p. 11.

and must bow their necks to the tyrants yoke."[73] Education became for the clergy the only conceivable bulwark against the "wicked and formidable machinery of papal and anti-republican despotism . . . the Hydra-monsters of civil and ecclesiastical tyranny."[74]

If despotic governments manipulated learning to inculcate fear, ministers knew that education must be the republic's primary stimulant of virtue. In guarding against both the right-wing attack of tyranny by king and bishop and against the equally despotic left-wing extreme of "licentious independence,"[75] clergymen envisioned defense plans for their own nation taking shape literally in a classroom of virtue. In an address to the students at Harvard in 1783, Charles Turner indicated the absolute necessity of education in achieving this end:

> . . . there is perhaps no one subject, which can more pertinently claim the attention of the people of these United States, at this time particularly, than that of education; and especially, the improvement of youth, in that christian practical godliness, public spirit and virtue, which would exclude the vile oppressing passions from their hearts; and form them, to that *true* spirit of liberty, which is nothing more nor less than a spirit of true christianity, considered as extending itself into, and operating in reference to matters of civil and ecclesiastical government and immunity. . . . But, if all the youth were educated, in the manner we recommend, *The Kingdom of God* would appear to have come, . . . and we might be induced to think of that *Millennial state,* the *approach* whereof, does perhaps at this time appear, by several prognostic symptoms, to be in some degree probable.[76]

By thus defining education as the means to liberty in both political and religious affairs, ministers tapped the concern for education which flowed from Puritan and repub-

73. Langdon, *The Republic of the Israelites,* p. 39.
74. Turner, *Due Glory to be Given to God,* p. 32.
75. Enos Hitchcock, *A Discourse on Education* . . . (Providence, 1785), p. 10.
76. Turner, *Due Glory to be Given to God,* p. 28.

lican springs. As citizens of a "confederate and Christian Republic,"[77] they had a twofold reason to uphold the priceless value of virtuous instruction. The critical role assigned to it, however, indicates that while New England continued to defend the supremacy of religion in society, spiritual values had become incorporated in a larger scheme of loyalty. The individual's confrontation with his Maker in religious experience and his interaction within the community of the redeemed became mediated by the political liberty and republican institutions which stood as the gospel's only sure foundation. In a profound sense Christ's kingdom became "of this world" as ministers advocated an educational ideal that coupled Christian and republican virtue.

The clearest evidence of this sanctifying of political values arises from a fourth dimension of clerical thought, the clergy's perceptions of and reactions to the rise of "infidelity."[78] With remarkable consistency New England ministers diagnosed rampant skepticism, irreligion, and atheism as basically a political disease. "The moment is come," announced Abiel Abbot on July 4, 1799, "when in our country, and in every Christian one, politics and religion are blended. The dagger is aimed at our government through our religion."[79] In focusing on the political consequences of rationalism, the clergy certainly gained considerable popular support for the beleaguered cause of orthodoxy.[80] Yet the political orientation of their argument can hardly be viewed only on these terms. By warning that "infidelity" was a frontal assault

77. David Tappan, *A Sermon Delivered to the First Congregation in Cambridge* . . . (Boston, 1793), p. 28.

78. Martin E. Marty, *The Infidel: Free Thought and American Religion* (Cleveland, 1961), pp. 19–58.

79. Abiel Abbot, *A Discourse, Delivered at North-Coventry* . . . (Hartford, 1799), p. 11.

80. Sidney Mead makes this argument in *The Lively Experiment,* pp. 52–53.

on the republic, New England preachers were expressing sensitivity not so much to public opinion as to the strong impulses of their own politicized theology.

As intellectual heirs of a tradition which had entwined republicanism and Christian theism, New Englanders in the last two decades of the century were unable to perceive religion as free from matters of civil government.[81] From ancient history they were convinced that "the state cannot stand without religion"[82] and from their own experience that "Rational Freedom cannot be preserved without the aid of Christianity."[83] As early as the closing days of their own Revolution they had described the promoter of "infidelity" as a false patriot "who contradicts and counteracts his own pretensions of love to his country."[84] One minister even suggested that having failed to thwart the founding of the republic, Satan had *"come down* to America, *in greater wrath,* and equal cunning" to accomplish the same goal by tempting the nation with wickedness.[85] From this perspective, the clergy viewed the sickly state of the church as symptomatic of tyranny's deadly infection.

In the 1790s this fear of political tyranny seemed to overshadow even ministers who equated Antichrist with "infidelity" rather than political oppression. The obser-

81. I am not arguing that it was novel for New Englanders to conceive of the political and religious realms as different functions of a larger reality. In the Revolutionary era, they were maintaining an age-old assumption that both of these were but means to the same end. This configuration of the civil and religious is new and significant, however, because its ultimate goal became characterized by the republican politics of the Revolution.

82. Nathan Strong, *A Sermon, Preached at the Annual Thanksgiving* . . . (Hartford, 1797), p. 13.

83. Timothy Dwight, *The Nature and Danger of Infidel Philosophy* . . . (New Haven, Conn., 1798), p. 89.

84. Nathan Williams, *A Sermon, Preached in the Audience of the General Assembly* . . . (Hartford, 1780), p. 14.

85. Turner, *Due Glory to be Given to God,* p. 17.

vation that the symbol of Antichrist could be "far more justly applied to the collective body of modern Infidels" at first suggests a retreat from an explicit civil millennialism; but a closer look reveals a change more apparent than real. Ministers came to attribute a demonic character to "infidelity" not because they perceived a change in Satan's ultimate goal of tyranny in church and state; but because they supposed he could destroy a Christian republic through heresy as effectively as through any political means. In pointing out the fatal flaw of French irreligion, Timothy Dwight declared that *"the liberty of Infidels was not the liberty of New England;* that France, instead of being free, merely changed through a series of tyrannies . . . [86] Likewise Chauncy Lee pictured French atheism as Satan's most devious scheme: it raised the unnerving question *"whether there be virtue enough in human nature to support a free Republican government."*[87] Abiel Abbot reasoned that the tyrants of France schemed to destroy American religion and thereby bring down the republic:

The immoralizing plan of the French is as systematic as their politics; it is a department of their politics. These French atheists in the country are not a few chance renegadoes [*sic*], whom adventure or curiosity has brought to our shores. That many of them are commissioned from the five apostles of atheism at Paris, who can doubt, if you consider their abilities and indefatigable industry and zeal? They have not sent men alone, but books to corrupt us. . . . In this manner has the faith of the United States been oppugned by that infamous production entitled 'the age of reason.' From what country did this issue? From France. Who wrote it? A jacobin American. Under whose auspices? Those of the Executive Directory.[88]

---

86. Timothy Dwight, *A Discourse on Some Events of the Last Century* . . . (New Haven, Conn., 1801), p. 33.

87. Chauncy Lee, *The Tree of Knowledge of Political Good and Evil* . . . (Bennington, Vt., 1800), p. 30.

88. Abbot, *A Discourse Delivered at North-Coventry*, pp. 12–13.

By these definitions heresy became the latest plot of unrestrained power against liberty.

In a profound sense politics had taken on a sacred
character. Even as New England pastors shook their
heads at the demise of religion, they observed in the
decline "a dagger aimed at our government through our
religion."[89] The spheres of church and state became
facets of a larger sacred purpose, the cause of liberty. At
the same time civil authority was being divested of church
control, it was acquiring larger purposes; while the
medieval union of church and state crumbled in the new
nation, New England espoused a higher form of "lay
investiture." The church deferred to the power of the
republic, having linked its aspirations to the rise of civil
and religious liberty that only the republic could ensure.
In New England thought, America did not assume "the
soul of a church" by some mysterious process of spontaneous generation. Yankees assigned a redemptive role
to the United States because the accepted canons of Christian republicanism, verified and made plausible by the
political scene both foreign and domestic, led them sys-
tematically to that conclusion.

℮

When Lyman Beecher wrote *A Plea for the West* in 1835,
he was convinced that the millennium would begin in
America. He traced this idea to his first encounter with
the writings of Jonathan Edwards. While the first spark
of Beecher's eschatological interest might well have been
struck by the author of *Some Thoughts Concerning the
Revival of Religion,* his ensuing interpretation shows
little resemblance to Edwards's apolitical millennialism.
Beecher firmly believed that the reign of Christ could not

89. Ibid., p. 11.

"come to pass under the existing civil organization of the nations." The continuation of arbitrary despotism and the predominance of feudal institutions demanded a "political emancipation," a series of revolutions that would champion "the cause of free institutions and the liberty of the world."[90] With the explicit assumption that the prosperity of the church hinged upon the status of civil government, Beecher boldly predicted the next advance of the kingdom: "the rapid and universal extension of civil and religious liberty, introductory to the triumphs of universal Christianity." For him, the next-to-the-last act of the cosmic drama had shifted to the stage of politics; "by the march of revolution and civil liberty, . . . the way of the Lord is to be prepared."[91]

It is hardly surprising that Beecher predicated God's renovating purpose for the world on the universal spread of civil and religious liberty; nor is it strange that his colleagues in the quest for revival and moral reform—men like Albert Barnes, Francis Wayland, and Alexander Campbell—likewise blended "the universal triumph of Christianity, and of civil and religious liberty."[92] What is surprising, however, is that recent publications that analyze the intellectual foundations of the "Evangelical

90. Lyman Beecher, "A Plea for the West," in *God's New Israel: Religious Interpretations of American Destiny,* ed. Conrad Cherry (Englewood Cliffs, N.J., 1971), pp. 119–20.

91. Ibid., pp. 119, 120. For another vivid example of the political focus of Beecher's religious concern, see his *Lectures on Political Atheism,* particularly 3, "The Perils of Atheism to the Nation" and 7, "The Republican Elements of the Old Testament," in Beecher's *Works,* 1 (Boston, 1852), 95–131, 176–90.

92. Albert Barnes, "The Position of the Christian Scholar," *Biblical Repository,* 3rd Ser., 6 (1850): 625. See also Francis Wayland, *The Duties of an American Citizen* (Boston, 1825), pp. 19–25; and Alexander Campbell, "Address on the Destiny of Our Country," in *Popular Lectures and Addresses* (Philadelphia, 1863), p. 174. Richard T. Hughes discusses Campbell's different route in arriving at conclusions similar to those of Congregational clergymen in "From Primitive Church to Civil Religion: The Millennial Odyssey of Alexander Campbell," *Journal of the American Academy of Religion* 44 (1976): 87–103.

Empire," have not gone beyond identifying republicanism either as an alien perspective competing with
millennialism or a parallel but unrelated influence.[93] The
deep-seated secular-religious dichotomy of the twentieth
century has blurred the ideas of ministers who knew no
such distinctions, making incomprehensible their republican eschatology. By thus separating into isolated components that which was developing as a coherent system
of thought throughout the eighteenth century, historians
have been insensitive to the explicit logic of ministers in
the Age of Jackson. From the premise that liberty both
civil and religious must precede the kingdom, the conclusion inevitably followed that the American republic, the
permanent seat of liberty, became "the primary agent of
God's meaningful activity in history."[94]

This was the precise argument on which Lyman
Beecher based his assumption that Christianity could not
flourish under despotic government:

But if it is by the march of revolution and civil liberty, that the way is to
be prepared, where shall the central energy be found, and from what
nation shall the renovating power go forth? What nation is so blessed
with such experimental knowledge of free institutions . . . ?[95]

---

93. Lois W. Banner has taken a significant step in identifying the importance
of republican thought for ministers in the early nineteenth century, but even she
has not gone beyond picturing millennialism and republicanism as two parallel
but separate modes of thought. See "Religious Benevolence as Social Control:
A Critique of an Interpretation," *Journal of American History* 60 (1973):
23–41, especially p. 35. William Gribben also emphasizes the importance of
republican ideology for nineteenth-century Protestant reform, but distin-
guishes sharply between secular and theocentric versions. The latter, he says,
was "a political extension of the country's scriptural tradition" and "reaf-
firmed the Judeo-Christian covenant tradition rather than the ideas of English
Commonwealthmen." In New England, at least, the terms of the covenant and
the ideas of Commonwealthmen have fewer differences than he appreciates.
See "Republicanism, Reform, and the Sense of Sin in Ante-Bellum America,"
Cithara 14 (1974): 25–41, quotations from p. 26.
94. Smylie, "National Ethos and the Church," p. 314.
95. Beecher, *A Plea for the West,* p. 120.

The obvious answer to these questions led Beecher to the same conclusion that Edwards had drawn a century before: "the millennium would commence in America."[96] God had created a new nation "itself free . . . to blow the trumpet and hold up the light."[97] Inspired by the full realization of freedom in America, the world would shortly be delivered from feudal ignorance and servitude. "The government of force will cease, . . . and virtue will take its place; and nation after nation cheered by our example, will follow in our footsteps, till the whole earth is free."[98] Beecher and Edwards thus stood on the same peak of expectancy awaiting crossing to the "Promised Land." But their ascent to this same vantage point had covered different intellectual terrain and had given them contrasting expectations as to how "Jordan" was to be forded. Beecher could survey the future with a confidence unknown to the pietists of the first Great Awakening, for he knew that in addition to the unpredictable forces of the revival which Edwards had marshaled, he had at his command the proven ally of republican liberty.[99]

96. Ibid., p. 120.
97. Lyman Beecher, *The Memory of Our Fathers*, in *Works* (Boston, 1852–1853), 2:176.
98. Beecher, *A Plea for the West*, p. 127.
99. An equally striking example of how civic the foundations of New England eschatology had become is the contrast between Jonathan Edwards's view of Antichrist and that of ministers after 1800. In 1748 Edwards refused to go along with the suggestion of the prominent Scottish evangelical William McColloch that the King of France might be the Antichrist. Edwards wrote to McColloch: "I can hardly think that this individual King of France or any other particular Prince in Europe, is what is chiefly intended by the Beast, so largely described in the 13th Chapter of Revelation, whose number is said to be six hundred and sixty-six." See Sereno E. Dwight, ed., *The Works of President Edwards with a Memoir of His Life*, 10 vols. (New York, 1829–1830), 1:264. Edwards's views are fully developed in Stephen J. Stein, "Cotton Mather and Jonathan Edwards on the Number of the Beast: Eighteenth Century Speculation about Antichrist," *Proceedings of the American Antiquarian Society* 134 (1975): 293–315. In contrast, New England ministers after 1800 were bold to name Napoleon and the French empire as the true successor of papal Antichrist. According to Thomas Andros of Berkley, Massachusetts, "The destruc-

   The civil religion that flowered during the Second
Great Awakening demonstrates the power of political
upheaval to color religious belief. During the French
Wars, the Revolution, and the founding of the Republic,
many of the clergy came to endow republican thought
with deep religious meaning. If de Tocqueville was right
that Americans in the Age of Jackson combined "the
notions of Christianity and of liberty so intimately" that
it was impossible "to make them conceive the one without the other,"[100] one certain reason was that for two
generations the week-to-week articulation of Christian
republicanism had convinced New Englanders that
America's divine election was a logical inference from her
commitment to liberty. "We may boast of our civil and
religious liberty;" observed Lyman Beecher, "but they
are the fruits of other men's labors."[101] While consciously expressing gratitude for the system of government which his generation inherited, Beecher surely did
not comprehend the full import of his words: he was
equally indebted to his forebears for a profound commitment to liberty as a sacred cause. Having been cham-

---

tion of the temporal power of the Pope has been followed by a scene of moral
corruption . . . Out of this vast moral chaos has arisen that willful king the true
antichrist, predicted by Daniel and St. John. . . . This absolutely lawless and
atheistic king, is the tyrant Napoleon" (*The Grand Era of Ruin to Nations
from Foreign Influence* [Boston, 1812], p. 8). At least a score of sermons prior
to the war of 1812 similarly indicted Bonaparte as the Antichrist. "This is the
era," complained one distraught pastor within months of Jefferson's Embargo,
"in which we hear a voice forbidding 'all men' excepting the vassals of the
'Beast' to buy or sell" (Elijah Parish, *Ruin or Separation from Antichrist*
[Portland, Maine, 1808], p. 8). See also John Baron, *Conjectures on
Prophecies* . . . (Boston, 1805), p. 27; William Fowler Miller, *A Dissertation
on the Harvest of Mystical Babylon* (Hartford, 1808), p. 11; Timothy Dwight,
A Discourse in Two Parts Delivered August 20, 1812 . . . (New York, 1812),
pp. 12–13; Freeman Parker, *A Sermon Delivered at Dresden, July 23,
1812* . . . (Portland, Maine, 1812), p. 11.
   100. Alexis de Tocqueville, *Democracy in America,* trans. Henry Reeve, 1
(New York, 1959), 317.
   101. Beecher, *Works,* 1:334.

pioned by New Englanders throughout the era of the
Revolution, this civil religion emerged with new vigor as
thousands of Yankees headed west advocating revivals,
foreign missions, and a cornucopia of moral reform. The
eighteenth-century tradition which had cast redemptive
history in terms of the cosmic advance of liberty and
decline of tyranny offered them—and the expanding
nation—a heritage that many proudly came to accept.
The sense of American mission and destiny which gave
focus to their vision is best understood, not as a product
of their own endeavors, but as a bequest by their
forefathers, whose republican accomplishment and
Christian faith they so greatly admired.

Note on the Printed Sermons of Massachusetts and Connecticut, 1740–1800

Thousands of sermons by hundreds of ministers from scores of towns across New England—this is the remarkable legacy of the Congregational clergy in the eighteenth century. In a culture that expected any minister worth his salt to exert influence beyond the four walls of his own meeting house, Yankee clergymen fired off sermons to the press at a rate that none of their Puritan forebears could match and unknowingly bequeathed a record which, taken as a whole, provides a significant opportunity to reconstruct the belief systems and perceptual frameworks of New England's Standing Order. Between 1740 and 1800, the clergy of Massachusetts and Connecticut alone published over eighteen hundred sermons in addition to other kinds of books and treatises.[1] But it is not merely the number of these thirty-to-fifty-page pamphlets that makes them so profitable. Two other considerations make them valuable as an index of social thought.

The most noticeable characteristic of this body of sermons is that it represents a broad sampling of what congre-

1. I was able to make this estimate by first identifying Congregational ministers using Frederick L. Weis, *The Colonial Churches and the Colonial Clergy of New England* (Lancaster, Mass., 1936); *Contributions of the Ecclesiastical History of Connecticut* (New Haven, Conn., 1861); *An Inventory of the Records of the Particular (Congregational) Churches of Massachusetts Gathered 1620–1805*, ed. Harold Field Worthley (Cambridge, Mass., 1970); and Joseph Clark, *A Historical Sketch of the Congregational Churches in Massachusetts* (Boston, 1858). The publications of each clergymen were then easily located in *National Index of American Imprints Through 1800: The Short-Title Evans,* ed. Clifford K. Shipton and James E. Mooney, 2 vols., (Barre, Mass., 1969).

gations all over New England were hearing regularly from the local pulpit. Of the thousand or so ministers who served churches in Massachusetts and Connecticut during these years, nearly half of them (481 of 1067 or 45.1 percent) broke into print at one time or another. Even more significant, nearly two-thirds of the Massachusetts and Connecticut congregations (322 of 477) sat under at least one publishing minister during these years.[2] While influential clergymen around Boston, New Haven, and Hartford did enjoy a direct access to the press, they by no means had a corner on it. Samuel Cooper of the prestigious Brattle Street Church in Boston, for instance, committed only a few of his sermons to the printer, while Joseph Lathrop of West Springfield, Massachusetts, became the most published Yale graduate of his day. John Adams's cousin Zabdiel likewise refused to allow the humble address of Lunenburg, Massachusetts (Worcester County), to impede his publishing ambitions. He joined a host of voices from the wilderness who considered it necessary during the Revolutionary era to present their ideas to a wider audience. This was a religious culture in which sermons circulated that were first heard in such towns as Great Barrington, Deerfield, Ashburnham, Plympton, Woodstock, Brooklyn, Darien, and Clinton. It is not surprising that New England's most famous eighteenth-century prophet spent his days thinking and writing in Northhampton and Stockbridge.[3]

2. The sources mentioned in note 1 also made it possible to locate the parish of a given minister.

3. Little is known about how many and what sort of persons bothered to read these sermons as pamphlets. My own hunch is that they served primarily as intramural communication within the ranks of the clergy. But that does not diminish their chief value to the historian, which is to discover what a broad spectrum of ministers found it useful to say to their local congregations week by week. It was normal procedure for Massachusetts to print enough copies of an election sermon to distribute to each minister in the province. See Rollo T. Silver, "Government Printing in Massachusetts Bay, 1700–1750," *Proceedings of the American Antiquarian Society* 68 (1958): 144–47.

It is easy to overlook the scattered origins of these sermons when one notes that a vast majority seems to have
issued from the presses of Boston, Hartford, and New Haven. At first glance, it appears that a few centrally located,
urban ministers used the power of the press to mold the
opinions of their rural colleagues. A more accurate picture, however, is that ministers throughout Massachusetts
and Connecticut, encouraged by their local constituents,
sought to gain a wider audience by having their sermons
printed in centers of influence.[4] Beyond their primary responsibility to their local congregations, Yankee ministers
tried to live up to another pressing obligation, that of
standing as moral guides and authoritative interpreters of
the mission of New England as a whole. The decentralized
polity of Congregationalists had always placed this burden squarely upon the shoulders of each minister, but the
various political tumults that raged during the last half of
the eighteenth century prompted more clergymen than
ever to address themselves "in a public manner" to the
issues of the day. It was no accident, for example, that the
production of sermons increased significantly during the
1770s and the 1790s. During the latter decade, when most
of America seemed to the Standing Order to be hell-bent
on destroying republican institutions and orthodox Christianity, clergymen in Connecticut and Massachusetts
flooded the press with 574 sermons, almost double the
number for any previous decade in New England history.[5]

4. The Selective Bibliography of Sermons includes each minister's town of
residence, which can easily be compared with the location of the sermon's
publication.
    5. During the 1790s the publication of fast and thanksgiving sermons
jumped to 160, four times the output of any previous decade. See William
DeLoss Love, *The Fast and Thanksgiving Days of New England* (Boston,
1895). The publication of Congregational sermons in Massachusetts and
Connecticut by decades is as follows: 1740s–249; 1750s–211; 1760s–240;
1770s–281; 1780s–231; 1790s–574.

That New England ministers in Revolutionary America "burst into print with merciless frequency" needs also to be understood as a function of pressure placed upon them by their own parishioners.[6] Hired and sustained by a local town and its church society, a member of the Standing Order had always been strictly dependent upon his constituents. In at least two respects the eighteenth century reinforced rather than relaxed this pressure from below. In the first place, the Great Awakening reversed the growing professional consciousness on the part of the clergy that J. William T. Youngs, Jr., has aptly called "Congregational clericalism." The revival forced ministers to keep a closer working relationship with those laymen who adhered to the dominant Congregational order.[7] Secondly, after 1745 Congregational laymen had their own compelling reasons to ensure that their pastor's viewpoints coincided with their own and that the church remained the ecclesiastical arm of the town. In an era of war and political strife, laymen might well have turned a deaf ear to theological debate, but they had every reason to listen with rapt attention when their minister rose to speak as a moral interpreter of politics. The pressures of the times actually forced community leaders to sponsor their clergymen as civic spokesmen: to build morale among the militia and the army, to bring comfort to the bereaved, to fortify the collective will on fast and thanksgiving days, to reconstruct a usable past for patriotic commemorations, to give benediction to weighty constitutional decisions, and, during the 1790s,

6. The phrase is that of Edmund S. Morgan in his review of Alan Heimert's *Religion and the American Mind from the Great Awakening to the Revolution* (Cambridge, Mass., 1966) in *William and Mary Quarterly*, 3rd ser. 24 (1967): 454.

7. J. William T. Youngs, Jr., *God's Messengers: Religious Leadership in Colonial New England, 1700–1750* (Baltimore, Md., 1976), pp. 92–141.

to convey the political doctrines of the Federalist party. While clergymen and local deacons bickered about such matters as clerical salaries, they continued to see eye to eye on a variety of issues related to local matters and the founding of the Republic.[8]

It was laymen, after all, who played a powerful role in determining just what sermons of a given minister would be published. As a matter of course New England legislatures initiated the printing of election sermons, but what is surprising is how many others went to press "at the desire of the hearers." The officers of militia companies not only invited certain ministers to address their troops but also decided if printing the sermon would be appropriate. Likewise, it was the organizing towns or committees that regularly saw to the publication of annual sermons commemorating the founding of Plymouth, the Boston Massacre, and the Battle of Lexington. The same pattern, furthermore, seems to obtain for a considerable number of fast and thanksgiving sermons, the largest single complement of sermons published in this period. The direct vote of a town meeting invited some ministers

8. In his extensive analysis of Concord, Massachusetts, Robert A. Gross offers a graphic example of how political crisis could forge a real, if uneasy, peace between contending factions within the town and could make even a clergyman as contentious as William Emerson an accepted community spokesman: "The Revolutionary crisis had brought a rare peace to his cantankerous flock. Now Emerson was expected to furnish spiritual guidance in his town's most difficult moment. He was ready for the task. He knew that his people's cause was the Lord's cause and that victory was certain if only they cleaved to their faith. And so he set out to rally his listeners against division and despair. They must stand in the days ahead a united and well-ordered community." *The Minutemen and Their World* (New York, 1976), pp. 21–29, 66–74, 108, 139, quotation on p. 72. Edward M. Cook, Jr., demonstrates the high correlation that existed in eighteenth-centuryNew England between civic and religious leadership. More than 60 percent of the 791 Congregational deacons who served in 106 churches in his sample towns were civic leaders as well; and 42 percent of the 3,032 selectmen elected between 1700 and 1784 appeared in the membership rolls of their local Congregational church. See "Town and Church," chapter 5 of *The Fathers of the Towns: Leadership and Community Structure in Eighteenth-Century New England* (Baltimore, 1976), pp. 119–41.

to make public particularly appropriate sermons;[9] more often, it was the "importunity" or the "strong desire" of some in the audience that singled out an address for broader distribution. Ebenezer Baldwin, for instance, explained that he was submitting his November, 1775, thanksgiving sermon for publication because many of his friends in Danbury, Connecticut "were impatient for a copy" and that "one Gentleman was so generous as to offer to defray the Expenses of printing it." The pressure seemed even greater upon Nathaniel Niles, who sent two sermons of June, 1774, to the printer with an apology for certain imperfections because a copy was "so suddenly called for."[10] Although less explicit in their descriptions of solicitation, most sermons of Revolutionary America were prefaced by some statement that it was strong audience approval that led to publication. While such an endorsement may have been partly a formality, any minister would certainly have thought twice about feigning his congregation's approval and then publishing abroad viewpoints that did not sit well at home. Congregations were willing to take on their pastors for much less serious affronts, as Jonathan Edwards could attest.

The great volume of sermons printed in Revolutionary America reflects anything but the arcane speculations of an isolated religious elite. The most likely sermons of all to be placed before the public were the very ones that received the heartiest "amen" among influential laymen. In other words, the printed sermons of Revolutionary New England are probably more representative of what was understood and believed in the pew than sermons

9. For an example of a town meeting voting in favor of publishing a thanksgiving sermon, see Joseph Lyman, *A Sermon Preached at Hatfield, December 15th, 1774* . . . (Boston, 1775).

10. Ebenezer Baldwin, *The Duty of Rejoicing under Calamities and Afflictions* . . . (New York, 1776); Nathaniel Niles, *Two Discourses on Liberty* . . . (Newburyport, Mass., 1774).

that failed to arouse anyone's interest and thus were buried quietly in a minister's dusty file of manuscripts. Clergymen, after all, were not alone in championing the sacred cause of liberty. "Will the Lion ever associate with the Lamb or the Leopard with the Kid," asked that strenuous Christian republican Samuel Adams, "till our favorite principles shall be universally established?"[11]

11. Adams to R. H. Lee, Boston, April 14, 1785, in *Writings of Samuel Adams,* ed. H. A. Cushing, vol. 4, p. 408. Pauline Maier emphasizes Adams's quest for liberty as a religous commitment in "Coming to Terms with Samuel Adams," *American Historical Review* 82 (1976):12–37.

Selective Bibliography of Sermons

I have attempted to make this bibliography useful by including a minister's town of residence in parentheses after his name; and after the place and date of publication, the number that the pamphlet is assigned in Charles Evans, *American Bibliography* . . . , 14 vols. (Worcester, Mass., 1903–1959) and in the microprint collection *Early American Imprints, 1639–1800,* ed. Clifford K. Shipton.

Abbot, Abiel (Haverhill, Mass.). *A Discourse, Delivered at North-Coventry* . . . Hartford, 1799. 35070.

———. *Traits of Resemblance in the People of the United States of America to Ancient Israel.* Haverhill, Mass., 1799. 35071.

Abbot, Hull (Charleston, Mass.). *The Duty of God's People to Pray for the Peace of Jerusalem* . . . Boston, 1746. 5724.

Adams, Amos (Roxbury, Mass.). *A Concise, Historical View* . . . Boston, 1769. 11130.

———. *The Expediency and Utility of War* . . . Boston, 1759. 8289.

———. *Religious Liberty an Invaluable Blessing* . . . Boston, 1768. 10810.

Adams, William (New London, Conn.). *A Discourse Delivered at New-London* . . . New London, Conn., 1761. 8779.

Adams, Zabdiel (Lunenburg, Mass.). *The Evil Designs of Men* . . . Boston, 1783. 17450.

———. *A Sermon Preached before His Excellency John Hancock* . . . Boston, 1782. 17807.

Allin, James (Brookline, Mass.). *Magistracy an Institution of Christ* . . . Boston, 1744. 5326.

Appleton, Nathaniel (Cambridge, Mass.). *A Sermon Preached October 9* . . . Boston, 1760. 8536.

———. *A Thanksgiving Sermon on the Total Repeal of the Stamp-Act.* Boston, 1766. 10230.

Austin, David (New Haven, Conn.). *The Millenial Door Thrown Open* . . . East-Windsor, Conn., 1799. 35128.

———. (Elizabethtown, N. J.). *The Millennium* . . . Elizabethtown, N. J., 1794. 26594.

Austin, Samuel (Worcester, Mass.). *Disinterested Love the Ornament of the Christian and the Duty of Man.* New York, 1791. 23135.

———. *A Sermon, Delivered at Worcester, on the Day of Public Thanksgiving* . . . Worcester, Mass., 1797. 31757.

Baldwin, Ebenezer (Danbury, Conn.). *The Duty of Rejoicing under Calamities and Afflictions* . . . New York, 1776. 14656.

Baldwin, Samuel (Hanover, Mass.). *A Sermon Preached at Plymouth, December 22, 1775.* Boston, 1776. 14657.

Ballantine, John (Westfield, Mass.). *The Importance of God's Presence with an Army* . . . Boston, 1756. 7615.

Barnard, Thomas (Salem, Mass.). *A Sermon Preached before His Excellency Francis Bernard* . . . Boston, 1763. 9334.

———. *A Sermon Preached to the Ancient and Honourable Artillery Company* . . . Boston, 1758. 8079.

Bascom, Jonathan (Eastham, Mass.). *A Sermon Preached at Eastham* . . . Boston, 1775. 13827.

Bean, Joseph (Wrentham, Mass.). *A Sermon Delivered at Wrentham, October 26, 1773* . . . Boston, 1773. 13136.

Belknap, Jeremy (Dover, N.H.). *An Election Sermon, Preached before the General Court of New-Hampshire* . . . Portsmouth, N.H., 1785. 18927.

———. (Boston), *A Sermon, Delivered on the 9th of May, 1798.* Boston, 1798. 33394.

Bellamy, Joseph (Bethlem, Conn.). *A Blow at the Root of the Refined Antinomianism of the Present Age.* Boston, 1763. 9339.

———. *An Essay on the Nature and Glory of the Gospel of Jesus Christ* . . . Boston, 1762. 9064.

———. *The Half-Way Covenant* . . . New Haven, Conn., 1769. 11171.

Bradford, Ebenezer (Rowley, Mass.). *The Nature and Manner of Giving Thanks to God, Illustrated.* Boston, 1795. 28339.

Brockway, Thomas (Lebanon, Conn.). *America Saved, or Divine Glory Displayed, in the Late War with Great Britain.* Hartford, 1784. 18383.

Brown, John (Cohassett, Mass.). *A Discourse Delivered on the Day of the Annual Provincial Thanksgiving* . . . Boston, 1771. 12001.

Burt, John (Bristol, Conn.). *The Mercy of God to His People* . . . Newport, R. I., 1759. 8312.

Buckminster, Joseph (Portsmouth, N.H.). *The Duty of Republican Citizens* . . . Portsmouth, N.H., 1796. 30132.

———. *A Discourse Delivered in the First Church of Christ at Portsmouth* . . . Portsmouth, N.H., 1784. 18385.

Byles, Mather (New London, Conn.). *A Sermon Delivered March 6th 1760* . . . New London, Conn., 1760. 8560.

Champion, Judah (Litchfield, Conn.). *A Brief View of the Distresses, Hardships and Dangers our Ancestors Encounter'd in Settling New-England* . . . Hartford, Conn., 1770. 11595.

Chandler, Samuel (Gloucester, Mass.). *A Sermon Preached at Gloucester, Thursday November 29, 1759* . . . Boston, 1759. 8316.

Channing, Henry (New London, Conn.). *The Consideration of Divine Goodness* . . . New London, Conn., 1794. 26755.

———. *God Admonishing His People of their Duty, as Parents and Masters.* New London, Conn., 1786. 19547.

Chauncy, Charles (Boston). *The Counsel of two Confederate Kings* . . . Boston, 1746. 5752.

———. *A Discourse on the Good News from a far Country.* Boston, 1766. 10255.

Checkley, Samuel (Boston). *The Duty of God's People when Engaged in War* . . . Boston, 1755. 7384.

———. *Prayer a Duty when God's People go Forth to War.* Boston, 1745. 5559.

Clarke, Jonas (Lexington, Mass.). *Fate of the Blood-Thristy Oppressors* . . . Boston, 1776. 14679.

Cogswell, James (Canterbury, Conn.). *God the Pious Soldier's Strength and Instructor* . . . Boston, 1757. 7874.

Conant, Sylvanus (Middleborough, Mass.). *An Anniversary Sermon Preached at Plymouth, December 23, 1776.* Boston, 1777. 15256.

Cooper, Samuel (Boston). *A Discourse on the Man of Sin.* Boston, 1774. 13227.

———. *A Sermon Preached before His Excellency John Hancock* . . . Boston, 1780. 16753.

Cooper, William (Boston). *The Honours of Christ Demanded of the Magistrate* . . . Boston, 1740. 4498.

Crane, John (Northbridge, Mass.). *A Sermon Preached at Northbridge November 27, 1800* . . . 37267.

Cumings, Henry (Billerica, Mass.). *A Sermon Preached at Billerica, December 15, 1796* . . . Boston, 1797. 32006.

Cushing, John (Ashburnham, Mass.). *A Discourse, Delivered at Ashburnham* . . . Leominster, Mass., 1796. 30306.

Dana, James (Wallingford, Conn). *A Sermon, Preached before the General Assembly* . . . Hartford, 1779. 16252.

Dwight, Timothy (New Haven). *The Duty of Americans at the Present Crisis* . . . New Haven, Conn., 1798. 33656.

———. *The Nature and Danger of Infidel Philosophy* . . . New Haven, Conn., 1798. 33657.

———. *The True Means of Establishing Public Happiness* . . . New Haven, Conn., 1795. 28610.

Eckley, Joseph (Boston). *A Sermon, Preached at the Request of the Ancient and Honorable Artillery Company* . . . Boston, 1792. 24287.

Eells, Nathaniel (Scituate, Mass.). *Religion is the Life of God's People* . . . Boston, 1743. 5173.

———. *The Great and Happy Doctrine of Liberty.* Boston, 1795. 29066.

Eliot, Jared (Killingworth, Conn.). *Give Caesar his Due* . . . New London, Conn., 1738. 4241.

———. *God's Marvellous Kindness* . . . New London, Conn., 1745. 5584.

Emerson, Joseph (Pepperrell, Mass.). *A Thanksgiving Sermon, Preached at Pepperrell* . . . Boston, 1766. 10293.

Emmons, Nathanael (Franklin, Mass.). *A Discourse, Delivered May 9, 1798* . . . Wrentham, Mass., 1798. 33674.

———. *A Discourse, Delivered November 3, 1790* . . . Providence, R. I., 1790. 22485.

———. *A Discourse Delivered on the National Fast, April 25, 1799.* Wrentham, Mass., 1799. 35444.

Fish, Elisha (Upton, Mass.). *Joy and Gladness; A Thanksgiving Discourse Preached in Upton, May 28, 1766* . . . Providence, R.I., 1767. 10612.

Fiske, Nathan (Brookfield, Mass.). *An Oration Delivered at Brookfield, Nov. 14, 1781* . . . Boston, 1781. 17153.

Fitch, Elijah (Hopkinton, Mass.). *A Discourse, the Substance of Which was Delivered at Hopkinton* . . . Boston, 1776. 14755.

Forbes, Eli (Brookfield, Mass.). *God the Strength and Salvation of His People* . . . Boston, 1761. 8855.

Foster, Dan (Windsor, Vt.). *An Election Sermon; Delivered before the Honorable Legislature of the State of Vermont* . . . Windsor, Vt., 1790. 22505.

Foxcroft, Thomas (Boston). *Grateful Reflections on the Signal Appearances of Divine Providence* ... Boston, 1760. 8599.
———. *A Seasonable Memento for New Year's Day.* Boston, 1747. 5947.
Frisbie, Levi (Ipswich, Mass.). *The Nature and Effects of the Works of Darkness* ... Newburyport, Mass., 1779. 35523.
———. *An Oration, Delivered at Ipswich* ... Boston, 1783. 17938.
———. *A Sermon Delivered February 19, 1795* ... Newburyport, Mass., 1795. 28716.
Goodrich, Elizur (Durham, Conn.). *The Principles of Civil Union and Happiness Considered and Recommended* ... Hartford, 1787. 20393.
Gordon, William (Roxbury, Mass.). *A Discourse Preached in the Morning of December 15th, 1774.* Boston, 1774. 14070.
Hart, Levi (Preston, Conn.). *Liberty Described and Recommended* ... Hartford, 1775. 14100.
Haven, Jason (Dedham, Mass.). *The Duty of Thanksgiving to God* ... Boston, 1759. 8366.
Haven, Samuel (Portsmouth, N.H.). *The Supreme Influence of the Son of God* ... Portsmouth, N.H., 1761. 8879.
Heminway, Jacob (East Haven, Conn.). *The Favour of God the Best Security of a People* ... New London, Conn., 1740. 4526.
Hilliard, Timothy (Barnstable, Mass.). *The Duty of a People under the Oppression of Man* ... Boston, 1774. 13329.
Hitchcock, Enos (Providence, R.I.). *A Discourse on Education* ... Providence, R.I., 1785. 19040.
Hitchcock, Gad (Pembroke, Mass.). *A Sermon Preached at Plymouth December 22d, 1774.* Boston, 1775. 14118.
———. *A Sermon Preached in the 2d Precinct in Pembroke* ... Boston, 1757. 7912.
Holmes, Abiel (Cambridge, Mass.). *A Sermon Preached at Brattle-Street Church* ... Boston, 1799. 35628.
Hopkins, Samuel (Newport, R.I.). *A Treatise on the Millennium.* Boston, 1793. 25635.
Howard, Simeon (Boston). *A Sermon Preached before the Honorable Council* ... Boston, 1780. 16800.
———. *A Sermon Preached to the Ancient and Honorable Artillery-Company* ... Boston, 1773. 12813.
Hunn, Nathaniel (Redding, Conn.). *The Welfare of a Government Considered.* New London, Conn., 1747. 5975.
Huntington, Joseph (Coventry, Conn.). *A Discourse ... on the*

Health and Happiness or Misery and Ruin, of the Body Politic in Similitude to that of the Natural Body. Hartford, 1781. 17190.

Hyde, Alvan (Lee, Mass.). *A Sermon Delivered at Lee, December 15th, 1796* ... Stockbridge, Mass., 1797. 32299.

Johnson, Stephen (Lyme, Conn.). *Some Important Observations, Occasioned by ... the Publick Fast* ... Newport, R.I., 1766. 10346.

Keteltas, Abraham (Newburyport, Mass.). *God Arising and Pleading His People's Cause* ... Newburyport, Mass., 1777. 15378.

———. (New York). *The Religious Soldier: or, the Military Character of King David* ... New York, 1759. 8383.

Langdon, Samuel (Cambridge, Mass.). *Government Corrupted by Vice, and Recovered by Righteousness.* Watertown, Mass., 1775. 14145.

———. (Portsmouth, N.H.). *Joy and Gratitude to God* ... Portsmouth, N.H., 1760. 8632.

———. *The Republic of the Israelites an Example to the American States.* Exeter, N.H., 1788. 21192.

Lathrop, John (Boston). *Innocent Blood Crying to God from the Streets of Boston* ... Boston, 1771. 12094.

———. *A Discourse on the Peace* ... Boston, 1784. 18551.

———. *A Discourse Preached December 15th, 1774* ... Boston, 1774. 13370.

Lathrop, Joseph (West Springfield, Mass.). *A Sermon, on the Dangers of the Times* ... Springfield, Mass., 1798. 33986.

Lee, Chauncy (Colebrook, Vt.). *The Tree of Knowledge of Political Good and Evil* ... Bennington, Vt., 1800. 37792.

Lee, Elias (Ridgefield, Conn.). *The Dissolution of Earthly Monarchies* ... Danbury, Conn., 1794. 27212.

Lowell, John (Newbury, Mass.). *The Advantages of God's Presence with His People in an Expedition Against their Enemies* ... Boston, 1755. 7452.

Maccarty, Thaddeus (Worcester, Mass.). *Praise to God, A Duty of Continual Obligation.* Worcester, Mass., 1776. 14830.

McClenachan, William (Blandford, Mass.). *The Christian Warrior.* Boston, 1745. 5622.

Macclintock, Samuel (Greenland, N.H.). *A Sermon Preached before the Honorable the Council* ... Portsmouth, N.H., 1784. 18567.

McKeen, Joseph (Beverly, Mass.). *A Sermon, Preached on the Public Fast* . . . Salem, 1793. 25746.

Marsh, Jonathan (Windsor, Conn.). *God's Fatherly Care of His Covenant Children* . . . New London, Conn., 1737. 4155.

Mather, Samuel (Boston). *The Fall of the Mighty Lamented.* Boston, 1738. 4276.

Mayhew, Jonathan (Boston). *A Sermon Preach'd in the Audience of His Excellency William Shirley* . . . Boston, 1754. 7256.

———. *The Snare Broken* . . . Boston, 1766. 10388.

———. *Two Discourses Delivered October 25th, 1759* . . . Boston, 1759. 8417.

Mellen, John (Lancaster, Mass.). *The Duty of All to be Ready for Future Impending Events* . . . Boston, 1756. 7719.

———. *A Sermon Preached in Billerica* . . . Boston, 1784. 18429.

———. *A Thanksgiving Sermon Preached at Billerica* . . . Boston, 1767. 10596.

Morrison, William (Londonderry, N.H.). *A Sermon, Delivered at Dover* . . . Exeter, N.H., 1792. 24563.

Morse, Jedidiah (Charlestown, Mass.). *The Present Situation of Other Nations of the World* . . . Boston, 1795. 29113.

———. *A Sermon, Delivered at the New North Church* . . . Boston, 1798. 34148.

Murray, John (Newburyport, R.I.). *Jerubbaal, or Tyranny's Grove Destroyed* . . . Newburyport, Mass., 1784. 18618.

———. *Nehemiah, or the Struggle for Liberty Never in Vain.* Newburyport, Mass., 1779. 16379.

Niles, Nathaniel (Newburyport, Mass.). *Two Discourses on Liberty* . . . Newburyport, Mass., 1774. 13502.

Niles, Samuel (Braintree, Mass.). *A Brief and Plain Essay on God's Wonder-Working Providence for New-England* . . . New London, Conn., 1747. 6037.

Osgood, David (Medford, Mass.). *The Devil Let Loose* . . . Boston, 1799. 36020.

———. *Some Facts Evincive* . . . Boston, 1798. 34284.

Parker, Samuel (Boston). *A Sermon, Preached Before His Honor the Lieutenant-Governor* . . . Boston, 1793. 25963.

Parsons, Jonathan (Newburyport, Mass.). *Freedom from Civil and Ecclesiastical Slavery* . . . Newburyport, Mass., 1774. 13513.

———. *Good News from a Far Country* . . . Portsmouth, N.H., 1756. 7746.

Patten, William (Hallifax, Mass.). *A Discourse Delivered at Hallifax* ... Boston, 1766. 10440.

Payson, Phillips (Chelsea, Mass.). *A Memorial of Lexington Battle* ... Boston, 1782. 17655.

Prentice, Thomas (Charlestown, Mass.). *The Vanity of Zeal for Fasts* ... Boston, 1748. 6227.

———. *When the People, and the Rulers among them, Willingly Offer Themselves to a Military Expedition* ... Boston, 1745. 5679.

Prince, Thomas (Boston). *God Destroyeth the Hope of Man!* Boston, 1751. 6766.

———. *The Salvations of God in 1746.* Boston, 1746. 5856.

———. *A Sermon Delivered at the South Church in Boston* ... Boston, 1746. 5857.

Sewall, Joseph (Boston). *The Lamb Slain* ... Boston, 1745. 5685.

Sherwood, Samuel (Weston, Conn.). *A Sermon, Containing Scriptural Instructions to Civil Rulers* ... New Haven, Conn., 1774. 13614.

———. *The Church's Flight into the Wilderness: An Address on the Times.* New York, 1776. 15082.

Stiles, Ezra (New Haven, Conn.). *The United States Elevated to Glory and Honor.* New Haven, Conn., 1783. 18198.

Stiles, Isaac (North Haven, Conn.). *The Character and Duty of Soldiers* ... New Haven, Conn., 1755. 7576.

———. *A Prospect of the City of Jerusalem* ... New London, Conn., 1742. 5066.

Street, Nicholas (East Haven, Conn.). *The American States Acting over the Part of the Children of Israel in the Wilderness* ... New Haven, Conn., 1777. 15604.

Strong, Cyprian (Chatham, Mass.). *God's Care of the New-England Colonies.* Hartford, 1777. 15606.

Strong, Nathan (Hartford). *The Agency and Providence of God Acknowledged* ... Hartford, 1780. 17002.

———. *Political Instruction from the Prophecies of God's Word* ... Hartford, 1798. 34612.

———. *A Sermon, Preached at the Annual Thanksgiving* ... Hartford, 1797. 32887.

Symmes, William (Andover, Mass.). *A Sermon, Delivered at Andover, December 1st, 1768.* Salem, 1769. 11487.

Tappan, David (Cambridge, Mass.). *Christian Thankfulness* ... Boston, 1795. 29604.

———. (Newbury, Mass.). *A Discourse Delivered at the Third Parish in Newbury* . . . Salem, 1783. 18203.

———. (Cambridge, Mass.). *A Discourse, Delivered to the Religious Society in Brattle-Street* . . . Boston, 1798. 34627.

———. *A Sermon, Delivered to the First Congregation in Cambridge* . . . Boston, 1793. 26244.

Thacher, Peter (Malden, Mass.). *An Oration Delivered at Watertown* . . . Watertown, Mass., 1776. 15101.

Throop, Benjamin (Norwich, Conn.). *A Thanksgiving Sermon, upon the Occasion of the Glorious News of the Repeal of the Stamp-Act* . . . New London, Conn., 1766. 10506.

Todd, Jonathan (East Guilford, Conn.). *Civil Rulers the Ministers of God for Good to Men.* New London, Conn., 1749. 6430.

Townsend, Jonathan (Medfield, Mass.). *Sorrow Turned into Joy.* Boston, 1760. 8750.

Trumbull, Benjamin (North Haven, Conn.). *God is to Praised for the Glory of His Majesty.* New Haven, Conn., 1784. 18812.

Tucker, John (Newbury, Mass.). *God's Goodness, Amidst His Afflictive Providences* . . . Boston, 1757. 8049.

Turner, Charles (Duxbury, Mass.). *Due Glory to be Given to God.* Boston, 1783. 18221.

———. *A Sermon, Preached at Plymouth, Dec. 22nd, 1773.* Boston, 1774. 13696.

Vinal, William (Newport, R.I.). *A Sermon on the Accursed Thing that Hinders Success and Victory in War* . . . Newport, R.I., 1755. 7583.

Wales, Samuel (New Haven, Conn.). *The Dangers of our National Prosperity* . . . Hartford, 1785. 19359.

Walter, Nathaniel (Roxbury, Mass.). *The Character of a Christian Hero.* Boston, 1746. 5877.

———. *The Character of a True Patriot.* Boston, 1745. 5706.

Webb, John (Boston). *The Government of Christ Considered and Applied.* Boston, 1738. 4321.

Webster, Samuel (Salisbury, Mass.). *The Misery and Duty of an Oppress'd and Enslaved People* . . . Boston, 1774. 13758.

Weld, Ezra (Braintree, Mass.). *A Discourse Delivered April 25, 1799* . . . Boston, 1799. 36699.

West, Samuel (Dartmouth, Mass.). *An Anniversary Sermon, Preached at Plymouth, December 22nd, 1777.* Boston, 1778. 16169.

———. *A Sermon Preached before the Honorable Council* . . . Boston, 1776. 15217.

Whitney, Josiah (Brooklyn, Conn.). *The Essential Requisites to form the Good Ruler's Character, Illustrated and Urged.* Hartford, 1788.   21601.

Whitney, Peter (Northboro, Mass.). *The Transgression of a Land Punished by a Multitude of Rulers.* Boston, 1774.   13769.

Whittelsey, Chauncy (New Haven, Conn.). *The Importance of Religion in the Civil Ruler, Considered.* New Haven, Conn., 1778.   16170.

Williams, Nathan (Tolland, Conn.). *A Sermon, Preached in the Audience of the General Assembly* . . . Hartford, 1780.   17072.

Williams, Samuel (Rutland, Vt.). *A Discourse Delivered before His Excellency Thomas Chittenden* . . . Rutland, Vt., 1794.   28093.

Williams, Solomon (Lebanon, Conn.). *The Duty of Christian Soldiers* . . . New London, Conn., 1755.   7596.

———. *The Relations of God's People to Him* . . . New London, Conn., 1760.   8770.

Williams, William (Weston, Mass.). *God the Strength of Rulers and People* . . . Boston, 1741.   4871.

Woodward, Samuel (Weston, Mass.). *The Help of the Lord* . . . Boston, 1779.   16685.

Worthington, William (Saybrook, Conn.). *The Duty of Rulers and Teachers in Unitedly Leading God's People* . . . New London, Conn., 1744.   5524.

Index

Abbot, Abiel, 169

Adams, John, 73, 94; *A Dissertation on the Canon and Feudal Law*, 48, 157, 165; on human nature, 136

Adams, Samuel, 74, 92, 93, 182

Adams, Zabdiel, 97, 113, 177

Ahlstrom, Sydney E., 4

American Revolution: impact on millennial ideas, 4–5, 22–23, 55–56, 88–90, 174; and Great Awakening, 25, 26, 26*n*, 70; and religion, 99*n;* as sign of the times, 148–49

Anarchy, fear of, 125, 132

Anglican Bishops, opposition to, 51, 74

Antichrist, 10, 11, 48, 70; as applied to other than Roman Catholic Church, 17, 87, 152–55; as civil tyranny, 17, 152–53; as British tyranny, 21–22, 24, 52, 86–87, 98, 131; Puritan interest in, 39; as France, 39–43, 47, 51, 52, 173*n;* as French infidelity, 133–34, 168–69; as Napoleon, 155, 155*n*, 173*n;* Jonathan Edwards on, 173*n*

"Apocalyptic whiggism," 144*n*

Appleton, Nathaniel, 41–42

Austin, David, 149, 150, 151, 152

"Babylon the Great," 40, 42, 153, 154. *See also* Antichrist

Bailyn, Bernard, 4, 57*n*, 99*n*, 114*n*, 145*n*

Baldwin, Alice M., 57*n*, 99*n*

Baldwin, Ebenezer, 66, 69*n*, 75, 87–88, 181

Banner, James M., Jr., 101, 135*n*, 137

Baptists, 8, 19, 149, 150*n*

Barnes, Albert, 171, 171*n*

Bavarian Illuminati, fear of conspiracy by, 130–32

"Beast, the," 42, 98, 153. *See also* Antichrist

Beecher, Lyman, millennial views of, 139, 144, 170–73

Belknap, Jeremy, 123, 124, 132, 151–52

Bellamy, Joseph, 35, 35*n*

Bercovitch, Sacvan, 4, 58*n*, 82*n*

Berger, Peter, 6*n*, 70*n*, 116*n*

Bernard, John, 45*n*

Bradford, Ebenezer, 135–36

Britain: tyranny of, as Antichrist, 21–22, 24, 52, 86–87, 98, 131; Jonathan Edwards's interest in, 32–33; clergy's pride in, 48–50, 53, 81–83; balanced constitution of, 65, 67, 83, 93; corruption of, 67–68, 70, 84, 85, 103; compared to ancient Egypt, 109–10, 120, 124

Buel, Richard, Jr., 101

Burgh, James, 59*n*, 95

Burr, Aaron, 33–35

Burt, John, 39

Burton, Asa, 112

Butterfield, Herbert, 3

Byles, Mather, 43

Campbell, Alexander, 171, 171*n*

Champion, Judah, 79

Christian History, The, 29, 30, 31

Civic humanism, 57, 58, 71*n*, 95, 137, 163*n*

Civil Religion, 140, 174–75; scholarship on, 140*n*

Civil War, English, 95

Clarke, Jonas, 121*n*

Cogswell, James, 21, 47

Turner, Charles, 69n, 71–72,
109, 118
Typology, 12, 16, 60; definition
of, 11n; and Israel, 16, 90, 96,
109, 128, 158–60; and Egypt,
109–10, 120, 124

Virtue, New England definitions
of, 66–67, 104–09 passim,
117, 137, 161, 163

Walpole, Sir Robert, 58n, 103
War: impact on religious belief,
4–5; 21–22, 36–44 passim,
55, 146
Warren, Joseph, 64, 77

Washington, George, 109,
124–25, 127
Wayland, Francis, 144, 171
Webster, Samuel, 56
West, Samuel, 1, 55, 59, 69n, 81,
86, 87, 158
Whiskey Rebellion, 124–25, 127
Whitefield, George, 32, 32n
Williams, Solomon, 38, 42
Winthrop, Hannah, 90n
Witherspoon, John, 63n
Wood, Gordon S., 4, 92n, 102n,
105n

Youngs, J. William T., Jr., 179